EDITION

PROPOSAL WRITING

Effective Grantsmanship

Soraya M. Coley
California State University, Bakersfield

Cynthia A. Scheinberg
Private Practice

Sage Sourcebooks for

the Human Services

Los Angeles | London | New Delhi
Singapore | Washington DC

Los Angeles | London | New Delhi
Singapore | Washington DC

FOR INFORMATION:

SAGE Publications, Inc.
2455 Teller Road
Thousand Oaks, California 91320
E-mail: order@sagepub.com

SAGE Publications Ltd.
1 Oliver's Yard
55 City Road
London, EC1Y 1SP
United Kingdom

SAGE Publications India Pvt. Ltd.
B 1/I 1 Mohan Cooperative Industrial Area
Mathura Road, New Delhi 110 044
India

SAGE Publications Asia-Pacific Pte. Ltd.
3 Church Street
#10-04 Samsung Hub
Singapore 049483

Acquisitions Editor: Kassie Graves
Editorial Assistant: Elizabeth Luizzi
Production Editor: Brittany Bauhaus
Copy Editor: Matthew Sullivan
Typesetter: Hurix Systems Pvt. Ltd.
Proofreader: Lori Newhouse
Indexer: Diggs Publication Services, Inc.
Cover Designer: Candice Harman
Marketing Manager: Lisa Sheldon Brown
Permissions Editor: Adele Hutchinson

Printed in the United States of America.

Library of Congress Cataloging-in-Publication Data

Coley, Soraya M. (Soraya Moore)
Proposal writing : effective grantsmanship /
Soraya M. Coley, California State University, Bakersfield, Cynthia A. Scheinberg, Private Practice. — Fourth Edition.

pages cm. — (SAGE sourcebooks for the human services)

Includes bibliographical references and index.

ISBN 978-1-4129-8899-5 (pbk.)

1. Proposal writing in human services. 2. Social service. I. Scheinberg, Cynthia A. II. Title.

HV41.C548 2013

658.15'224—dc23

2012039721

This book is printed on acid-free paper.

SUSTAINABLE FORESTRY INITIATIVE
Certified Chain of Custody
Promoting Sustainable Forestry
www.sfiprogram.org
SFI-01268
SFI label applies to text stock

13 14 15 16 17 10 9 8 7 6 5 4 3 2 1

PROPOSAL
WRITING

4

EDITION

SAGE SOURCEBOOKS FOR
THE HUMAN SERVICES SERIES

Series Editors: ARMAND LAUFFER and CHARLES GARVIN

Contents

List of Figures

List of Tables

Preface to the Fourth Edition

This book is written to assist a beginning grant writer in a non-profit agency or organization seeking to fund community services and programs, and for students preparing to go into the "helping professions." In fact, the book was initially conceived while we were teaching program design and proposal writing at California State University, Fullerton. We felt that we wanted to de-mystify the grant writing process and provide a guide to writing that was as jargon-free and as simple to use as possible. The book is not an exhaustive text on proposal writing as its focus is to provide a solid foundation on which to add years of experience to fine-tune grant writing skills. We are pleased to be asked to prepare a fourth edition of *Proposal Writing*.

The feedback that we have received from those of you who use the book as a text is very gratifying. We always struggle to include as many of the great suggestions we receive while keeping the book short and clear. This fourth edition includes most of the new suggestions we received, and we sincerely hope that we have made the book even more useful to you! We also will update the accompanying website with more examples.

We are indebted to the following individuals who provided us with thoughtful reviews of the third edition: Darla Beaty, University of Houston; Bari Cornet, University of California, Berkeley; Charlie Grose, Wayne State University; Michael Holosko, University of Georgia; David Moxley, University of Oklahoma; Holly Riffe, Northern Kentucky University; and Katherine Selber, Texas State University. We have attempted to integrate as many of their suggestions as possible into the text while keeping the book true to its intended "beginning writer" audience.

As we finish this fourth edition, the U.S. economy continues to struggle, and many international markets are weak. There is a raging debate about the role of the government and the effective mix of public and private strategies to address basic human and community needs. There are strong competing priorities for limited funding opportunities. It is truly a difficult time for community programs and for grant writers who struggle to find funding and, when they do, to win those grants. Funding priorities continue to shift, human service programs continue to come in and out of focus, while community needs continue to grow. If it weren't for the unique people who see these needs and respond, the world would be far worse off. It is a privilege to contribute to the betterment of our society by helping people to obtain funding to help others. Over the years, we have found copies of our little book on Native American reservations, in small rural town libraries, and abroad. In each instance, we were deeply moved to realize that people everywhere were grappling with tenacious social issues and working for change. This book is dedicated to you, the grant writer, change agent, community activist, caring person . . . may you have the joy of creating a symphony of service and the exhilaration of hearing that symphony played in your community.

We have many people to thank for their support of this fourth edition, specifically, Ron Coley for his unending support; Lietta M. Wood for her encouragement; Dr. Horace Mitchell, President of California State University, Bakersfield, for his support of the completion of the book; and the faculty, staff, and students at CSUB who provided the inspiration for a timely completion. We appreciate the reviewers who reaffirmed that we were meeting a need in the world of grant writing and fund development. A special thank you also goes to Maricela Guerra for her research assistance. We also thank our editor, Kassie Graves, for her support and patience as we extended the due date to meet unforeseen personal challenges and work obligations. Thank you.

To Ron Coley, my husband, who supported me in all stages of this book; and who had faith when I faltered, praise and inspiration when I doubted, and love and friendship always. —S. C.
and
I dedicate this fourth edition to my granddaughter, Maya, and grandson, Kai, who inspire great hope for a beautiful future. —C. S.

Chapter One

An Orientation to Proposal Writing

A Book for a Beginning Grant Writer

There is nothing more exciting or gratifying than to participate in designing a program, writing a proposal, and, ultimately, seeing that program come to life in the community! Writing an effective grant is both an art and a science—it requires a focus on the details of project implementation and proposal assembly, as well as knowing how the project will help a client and make an impact on the community. It can be a very intimidating process.

1

This book is written to help the beginning grant writer. This is not a book for an experienced grant writer seeking to fine-tune skills or for individuals seeking to write research proposals, as the components of these proposals are quite different. In these pages, you will find a basic guide to assist you as a novice grant writer—perhaps you are a student planning a career in the helping profession or a staff member of a non-profit agency asked to write your first grant to meet a need in the community. There is minimal use of jargon in the book so that the book can be a friendly companion as it takes you step-by-step through the process of writing a proposal for a non-profit organization seeking public, private, or corporate funding.

A Brief History of Giving and Philanthropy

The Greek word *philanthropia* is defined roughly as "love for mankind" ("Philanthropy," n.d.). Throughout history, individuals have found a way to help others in need. We believe the urge to give, or to be philanthropic, in the face of need is universal.

The history of giving in the United States has its roots in the 16th-century Elizabethan Poor Laws of England that "were administered through parish overseers, who provided relief for the aged, sick, and infant poor, as well as work for the able-bodied in workhouses" ("Poor Law," 2012). Under the Poor Laws, persons who were needy through no fault of their own—such as the elderly, the sick, widows with children, and orphans—were cared for, while those who were needy but viewed as having caused their needs, or who were perceived as being able to address their needs without assistance, were ignored. The ignored population included older children/young adults, pregnant single mothers, thieves, and other criminals.

The Puritans followed the Elizabethan Poor Law model in caring for needy members in the community and took up collections in the parishes to meet those needs. Throughout much of U.S. history, benevolent associations were created as a kind of community-based insurance plan where individuals joined the association and paid dues that were used to help a family with illness or the costs of burial. These associations were established along the lines of ethnicity, employment, or religious affiliation.

The first grants made by the U.S. government were land grants providing the opportunity for needy citizens to obtain property on which to build a home and put down roots. Bounty Land Warrants were provided to soldiers in the Revolutionary War in lieu of financial compensation. The Morrill Act of 1862 provided 30,000 acres of land for each congressional district that resulted in the creation of 69 colleges such as Cornell University and Massachusetts Institute of Technology.

The late 1800s and early 1900s marked a period of explosive growth in strategies to meet community needs. In 1889, Jane Addams founded Hull House, a settlement house that accepted needy men, women, and children, and provided a range of services on site, including client advocacy for improved schools and services. Jane Addams and Hull House mark the beginning of social work as a profession in the United States. Because it is fitting to see how seriously impacted the non-profit sector is right now, we are including this excerpt on Hull House from a *Chicago Tribune* article from January 2012:

> Jane Addams Hull House Association will be out of business Friday, leaving employees and clients scrambling to fill a void the 122-year-old organization will leave. Despite announcing last week plans to close in March, board Chairman Stephen Saunders said Wednesday that the organization will fold this week because it can no longer afford to stay open. He also said Hull House plans to file Friday for bankruptcy.
>
> With government funding taking a hit and the need for services climbing, Hull House's revenue dropped from $40 million in 2001 to just $23 million in June. "We could not possibly raise enough money to sustain the organization," Saunders said. (Thayer, 2012)

In the early 1900s, the first charitable foundations came into being: the Carnegie Foundation was founded in 1905 to promote education. Shortly thereafter, in response to a feeling that he wanted to do something good with his money, John D. Rockefeller, Sr., established the Rockefeller Foundation in 1913 with a mission to promote the well-being of humanity around the world. These big foundations were created out of the wealth of individuals, and so it is today with individual, family, and corporate foundations created to give back to the community per the desire and specifications of the creator.

In 1913, the U.S. government began collecting income taxes, and grants were made by the federal government to address critical needs and disasters. By 1933, the country was well into the Great Depression under Republican President Herbert Hoover who believed that the depression would eventually be resolved by "trickle-down" economics, when the Democratic President Franklin Delano Roosevelt (FDR) was elected into office. Through two terms in office, he created a New Deal with numerous programs: Social Security, the Federal Deposit Insurance Corporation, the Securities and Exchange Commission, and the National Labor Relations Board. A plethora of work programs were launched to aid in employment such as the Works Progress Administration and the Civilian Conservation Corps. These social programs provided work for the unemployed, put food on the family table, and spurred the development of a robust infra-structure of roads, bridges, dams, and other public works.

The next burst of social programs on the scene came in the 1960s under the Democratic President Lyndon B. Johnson's "Great Society," which ini-tiated a flurry of social programs, including those to address racial injustice and begin the so-called "War on Poverty." As you can see, particular social issues come in and out of style and face reductions or increases in funding based on the politics of the day. There is true vulnerability in the world of giving. It is subject to the vagaries of politics, the transfer and maintenance of social power, wealth, and religious beliefs.

Today, there is a huge array of both public and private funders offering grants. In 2002, in an effort to streamline access to and the submission of grants to the federal government, a portal called Grants.gov was established as a central storehouse for information on over 1,000 grant programs and approximately $500 billion in annual awards offered in 21 categories by the 26 federal grant-making agencies.

Table 1.1   21 Categories of Federal Grant-Making

Agriculture	Arts	Business and Commerce	Community Development
Disaster Prevention and Relief	Education	Employment	Labor and Training
Energy	Environmental Quality	Food and Nutrition	Health
Housing	Humanities	Information and Statistics	Law, Justice, and Legal Services
National Resources Recovery Act	Regional Development	Science and Technology	Social Services and Income Security
Transportation			

About the Non-Profit Agency

The non-profit agency (also commonly known as the *public charity*, the *not-for-profit organization* or *agency*, or the *non-governmental organization*) is usually established in response or reaction to a particular community need or issue. In its most simple form, the agency is created by a group of citizens who gather together, agree certain services are needed, write a mission statement, create a board of directors and bylaws and submit an application to the IRS for determination on their non-profit status. Since 1913, agencies that are established for public benefit receive a designation of 501(c)3 through the Internal Revenue Code, enabling organizations to focus on the public benefit and not pay tax on their income. There is a common misunderstanding that a non-profit organization cannot make a profit. It can and, if it is going to be a viable business, it must! This tax designation allows the agency to avoid taxation on its profits. It pays regular payroll taxes on employees, sales tax on purchases, sales tax on items sold, and, in many cases, property taxes. From the moment of its birth, the non-profit agency is on a search for funds to enact its mission in the community. The following are some ways in which non-profit agencies generate revenue:

- *Events* such as dinners, auctions, picnics, dances, or pledge drives to raise money
- *Donors* or those individuals who contribute financially to the agency
- *Corporate donors* who give funds through a grant process
- *Products* the agency creates and then sells such as educational brochures or booklets
- *Clients* who may contribute financially to the agency by paying a reduced fee-for-service
- *Businesses* the agency run that further their mission and generate an income
- *Grants and contracts* from local government, state government, or federal governmental offices

Most agencies will receive the bulk of their income through grants and contracts, with their annual budget looking somewhat like the pie chart below:

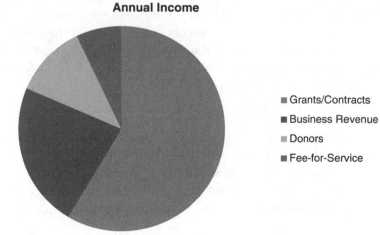

Figure 1.1   Sources of Agency Income

Each source of potential funding has its own rules and expectations in relation to the types of programs it will fund, how it will receive requests for funding, and the style of the proposal or application it will accept. The process of seeking funding for the non-profit agency opens the door to a rich and fascinating funding world that may include tapping into the altruistic drives of individual donors, following the vagaries of politics to understand and tap in to governmental funding, and seeking to develop partnerships to access the wealth and influence of private foundations. The proposal carries the expression of community need to the funder and, if successful, results in a contract for services, a grant-in-aid, or, simply, a grant.

Differences between Grants and Contracts

To make some initial terms clear, the process of writing a proposal for funding has come to be known as *grant writing*, and the individual(s) responsible for the writing of the proposal is a *grant writer*. The entity providing the money is called the *funder*. While it is commonly said that one writes a proposal to obtain a *grant*, it may be that the end result is actually a *contract*.

Contracts for services or, *fee-for-service contracts* as they are often called, require the agency to provide services on behalf of a funder; the agency is reimbursed on units of service delivered. For example, a community dental clinic has successfully won a contract with the county to provide dental care to low-income children. The multi-page document signed by the agency and the county will spell out the details of the contract and include a description of the services to be delivered. In this example, the contract states that the clinic will be reimbursed a specified amount per amalgam filling 100 units at $30/unit, per crown 10 units at $400 per unit, and per cleaning 100 units at $40 per unit. The clinic bills the county in arrears (after the delivery of services) of service provided. If the clinic does not need five of the 10 units of crowns in the contract, they will most likely need to make a modification on the contract or risk losing this amount from the contract. In general, a contract requires a great deal of management to ensure that all services are delivered appropriately, services are billed and reimbursed appropriately, and timely changes are made to the contract to ensure full use of the funds.

On the other hand, this same clinic has also received a grant from the CSM Foundation, a corporate funder in the community. The terms of the corporate grant are that the agency will provide dental care to 100 low-income children. The agency will receive the full amount of the grant at the beginning of the fiscal year and will report its progress to the foundation. It is generally true that grants are more flexible and require a less detailed account of services than contracts.

There are different funders for different funding needs, including governmental, corporate, or community foundations as well as small family foundation funders. We will address each type of funding, from how to locate funding sources to how to respond to their request for proposals (RFP). Most people find the state or federal proposal the most challenging to write. We will focus on how to conceptualize a project and write a proposal for a state and federal funder in the belief that the skills you will learn to accomplish this task will be transferrable to the preparation of a foundation or corporate proposal.

Funding Sources and Guidelines for Grants and Contracts

Most funding sources have missions or mandates to follow. In the case of governmental entities, the mandates are developed through legislative process and administered by the governmental agency; the resultant funding is allocated to address the identified need. Corporations and foundations may exist to meet certain needs, such as health foundations that were developed out of the transition from non-profit status to for-profit structures. Other corporations may target particular issue areas they want to address, such as youth, education, or domestic violence.

Most funders want something in return for their giving. In some cases, this may be increased visibility and goodwill in a local community; in others, perhaps giving leads to increased revenue. An example of this type of strategy can be seen in credit card use linked to charitable giving. If you use X card, the charity will receive a percent of your total purchase. Corporations are likely to view proposals favorably if they meet their own internal needs or promote the corporate image in the community. When writing these proposals, be aware of the WIFM rule—"What's in it for me?"—and design a program with clear benefits to the corporation and the agency/organization, but also, most importantly, to those you are serving.

Governmental versus Foundation Applications

When governmental agencies have available funds, they issue a *funding announcement*, which provides the information needed to obtain a *request for applications*, abbreviated as RFA, or *request for proposals*, or RFP. (We recently saw a funder put out an RFS or *request for services*.) This RFA/RFP is the application packet containing full instructions and all of the required forms needed to submit the proposal. Funding announcements for the federal government can be found on the Grants.gov website or in publications such as the Federal Register, or at the websites for particular governmental agencies. There are many governmental offices issuing funding announcements, such as the Department of Health and Human Services and the Centers for Disease Control. (See Appendix B: Funding Resource Information.)

Federal government applications are generally prepared online through Grants.gov, which requires the agency to be pre-registered on the site. This process takes about two weeks to complete, and, once completed, any number of proposals can be submitted and tracked through the site. State or county government applications vary in their processes, with some using online and others requesting paper applications.

In some cases, foundations may not issue formal RFA/RFPs; instead, they will identify those agencies in the community eligible to be considered for funding and invite them to apply. In addition to a well-written proposal, foundations give consideration to other factors in their decision-making process. We surveyed 164 foundations that ranked these as the top factors affecting whether an agency gets funded:

- Demonstrates a positive and measurable impact on those being served
- Is a collaborative or partnership
- Indicates a cost-effective operation
- Supports other organizations in the community
- Reflects cultural sensitivity and diversity
- Focuses on primary prevention of the problem
- Has a proven track record
- Establishes new, innovative programs
- Receives funding from other sources
- Has previous relationship with foundation
- Has a not-too-radical reputation
- Has competent and professionally trained staff

In addition, the foundations revealed that two of the most common weaknesses in proposals are (1) not clearly identifying and substantiating a significant problem and (2) a lack of clarity as to how funds are to be expended for project activities.

The guidelines for the submission of foundation applications are typically found on the respective foundations' websites or through a variety of efforts such as the "Foundation Directory Online" offered by subscription through the Foundation Center (New York) (fconline.foundationcenter. org). Foundations generally receive proposals two to four times per year, and some foundations accept proposals by invitation only. Foundations may focus their giving on local or regional levels (e.g., Southern California), while others are national in scope.

The Proposal Submission and Scoring Processes

There are several steps involved in submitting a proposal. This process is illustrated in Figure 1.2.

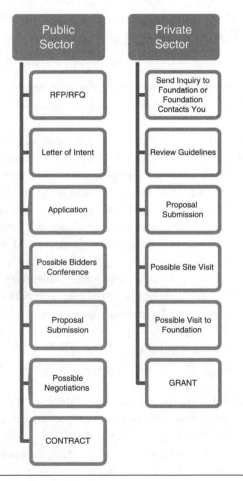

Figure 1.2   The Funding Process

Most governmental funders and many foundations require a potential applicant to submit a *letter of intent* to apply for funding. In this letter, an applicant is asked to briefly describe the project and the agency. These letters are often used to ensure that the applicants are submitting a proposal within the scope of the funder's request. The applicants will receive a return letter from the funder giving permission and instructions as to how to proceed with a full application (or thanking the applicants for their interest). The applicants will be notified as to the dates and locations of any *bidder's conferences* designed to enhance the understanding of the goals of the funder and of specific details in proposal preparation. The bidder's conference provides the funder with the opportunity to clarify the intent of the proposal and answer questions about the proposal in as fair a manner as possible. Prospective applicants receive a written transcript of the proceedings of all of the conferences held by the funder and of any questions they have answered over the phone. This provides a level playing field where all applicants have the same information. The conference also provides an opportunity to learn what other agencies are interested in submitting an application, leading to possible cooperative proposals and assessment of the competition. It is customary for the funder to provide attendees a roster of all attendees at the bidder's conference.

The proposal must be received by the potential funder by the deadline. Submission deadlines will be included in the announcement and will determine the time frame for proposal preparation. Many governmental funders allow approximately four to six weeks between the funding announcement and the proposal due date. Funders are very serious about submission due dates, and we are aware of many sad stories of agency personnel running the grant into the office at one minute after the due date and being turned away.

An additional step in the proposal process is when the federal government requires that the applicants notify the state government about the funding request they are making. In this case, instructions are also in the application packet and describe who to make contact with and when. (This is sometimes called a *single point of contact* request or SPOC.) It may suffice to send a copy of the proposal to the SPOC when the application is submitted to the federal office. We also recommend that you send a copy to your local legislators so they might advocate on your behalf.

Once the proposal is submitted and has undergone a preliminary review, some funders will make site visits to meet the board, executive director, and staff members to ensure that the agency is doing what it has indicated in the proposal. In some cases, the agency may be invited to make a presentation to the grantor's board of directors or staff.

Proposal Scoring

There is no single approach used for proposal scoring. Typically, government funding agencies use a weighting system when reviewing proposals, with various weights or points assigned to each section of the proposal. The review criteria and the weighting system to be used are sometimes listed in the agency's program announcements or application packets. Foundations and corporations identify their proposal evaluation criteria through funding announcements, but are less likely to indicate the point values assigned to specific proposal sections.

In reviewing the proposal scoring criteria used by public and private funders supporting human service programs, we found they generally weighted the proposal sections in the following order:

1. Project approach including goals, outcomes, and project activities

2. Need/problem statement

3. Budget

4. Agency capability

5. Evaluation methods

Funders are looking for projects that are realistic, that have measurable outcomes with a good chance for success, and that are ambitious. It is always attractive if the program reaches beyond known boundaries into unknown or untried arenas, which, if successful, will be a step into the future for the organization (and a nice feather in the cap of the funder).

Many times, one "well-placed" proposal has a greater possibility of being funded than one scattered indiscriminately to a variety of funders (also known as *shot-gunning*). Foundation and corporate development consultants are in contact with one another and are aware of a proposal that has been circulated in this manner and look less favorably on it.

A notification of award is usually mailed by the funder to the applicant, and in some cases, the successful applicant may be contacted in advance by phone. In cases where the application is rejected and the proposal not funded, it is often possible to receive the scoring and reviewers comments. This is very helpful and strongly encouraged. On occasion, an agency may contest the outcome of the application process. Most governmental funders have a grievance process to follow if the applicant believes there is an error or oversight or seeks to contest the determination. Details regarding this process will be found in the RFA packet.

In the best case, an award letter will arrive, indicating that the application was successful and announcing the award amount. Sometimes this amount is less than applied for, and applicants will enter into negotiations with the funder. During these negotiations, the project description and the budget sections of the proposal will be modified to reflect the level of effort required under the funded amount.

Chapter Two

Organizing the Writing and Using Technology

The Nuts and Bolts of Writing a Proposal

The following section addresses some of the issues associated with general organization and work habits. Individuals who have written proposals before will be very aware of the usual obstacles and barriers that greet the writer along the way. As most proposals are written under the pressure of deadlines (which are almost always too short), organization becomes critical.

In today's climate, proposals are most often prepared by more than one person. If the proposal is being written by a collaborative or partnership, there may be one administrator and a grant writer from the lead agency, and one or two others from participating agencies. If a sole agency is writing the proposal, there may be a grant writer, an executive director, a program director, and program staff involved in the writing. Whatever the configuration, there is usually one main writer. This "point" person pulls it all together into one style, ensures that all of the extra materials are gathered up for inclusion into the grant, and makes certain that the grant application is in the format required by the funder. It will be the job of the main writer to read the RFA carefully and in minute detail to find the technical aspects of the proposal preparation such as font size, margins, page limitations, and page numbering.

As many things begin to happen simultaneously in the writing process, we can't over-emphasize the need for a place to work that allows for the undisturbed storage of materials. Think of what it is like to write a term paper—your research is spread out on the table, your drafts are piled up next to it, and your books are spread open on the floor. When writing the proposal, you may have a pile for the data related to the problem, one for work plans from your agency and other agencies (if collaborating), a section for budgets, and support letters or other documentation from each participating agency. Many people we know use boxes to contain the components of a particular project, while others use notebooks.

It is most helpful to have someone edit your proposal. In most cases, this will be someone who has worked with the grant writer in preparing the proposal so there is familiarity with the project. The editor will help to ensure that the main ideas in the proposal are clearly stated and that the proposal is internally consistent. All of the numerical totals in budgets should be double-checked by the editor as well. Finally, the editor will double-check to ensure that all attachments are included and the proposal is assembled accurately.

Although we have mentioned timelines that are imposed by the funder, the grant writer must also be aware of other processes the grant application must pass through before being ready for submission, such as approval by the board of directors of the agency and partner agencies.

It is worth the time and energy it takes to ensure adequate supplies for the writing process in advance. Purchase extra paper (printer, fax, and copier), copier toner, printer ink, stamps, large envelopes, white-out, file folders, index cards, pens, and large butterfly clips. Have overnight express mailing pre-addressed and stamped in preparation for a last-minute rush. Know where you can go to use a copier if yours breaks at the last minute, AND ALWAYS BACK UP YOUR WORK. (Remember to scan for viruses every time electronic media changes hands from one writer to another source.)

Finally, make sure you have a copy of the final proposal—not just on your computer, but a hard copy as well.

Fifty percent of the proposals funded are re-submissions that were denied the first time. This statement is not made to discourage you, but rather to ground you a bit in the reality of the process. Because this is a highly competitive business, grant writers learn not to take rejection personally. In fact, too much personal investment in the proposal can work to your disadvantage, as you may lose the objectivity needed to negotiate the proposal, make modifications, or even learn from mistakes.

Writing for an Established versus New Organization

There is a vast difference in approach if you are writing for an established organization or starting your own venture. An established organization has the clear competitive advantage, as it has a history in the community, has developed a successful funding track record, and has an established board of directors, programs, and staff. These are huge features to overcome in a newly formed not-for-profit entity. If you are venturing out on your own, there are a number of features you will want to consider when writing your first proposal:

1. *Consider linking your program to an existing non-profit* with a similar mission. Meet with the executive director and explore the possible fit. Develop a contractual agreement that spells out your relationship to the agency to protect your ideas and employability in the project once funded. Then, write the proposal and use the existing agency's track record to achieve success!

2. *Involve persons in the project who have obtained and managed grants or contracts* over their careers, and use their experience and successes to build a credible foundation for your new entity. This will help to demonstrate that you have the capacity to manage a grant project and the capability to implement the program you are proposing.

3. *Talk to the staff at the foundation you want to work with.* Make sure that your ideas are a good fit and that the foundation will consider a "first" proposal.

4. *Clearly demonstrate the support for your proposal.* You must have solid commitments from partner agencies as well as from the community you intend to serve. This is always an important feature but becomes even more important in this case as you must prove that the intended recipients of the services actually want and will use the services.

5. *Have an experienced grant writer review your work.* Consult as needed with staff in similar programs. Listen and learn from their experiences and build this knowledge base into the proposal. This will demonstrate to the funder that you realize that there are programs similar to yours and that you are willing to learn from them rather than reinvent the wheel.

6. *Don't under-sell the project* and set yourself up for failure and frustration. Use care in developing your budget. You will want to come in "on target" with the budget request. If the budget is unrealistic, you will likely not be considered for funding.

7. *Realize that your passion to start something new is both a blessing and a curse.* The same enthusiasm that will endear you to some will cause others to shun you because, usually, passionate people don't listen. Be willing to see your idea morph into something similar but also different from the original. Be willing to compromise to reach your goals. Remember, this will be your first program, and you can continue to build the dream over time.

Writing for an Established Agency

If you are writing for an established agency, chances are good that you will be working in a small writing group or, at least, will need to obtain pieces of the proposal from others within the organization. The following ideas may be helpful to you in guiding the group grant writing process:

1. Establish the writing timeline early in the process and provide "due dates" to all involved. Make the date earlier than is actually needed to allow you time to bring it all together.

2. Establish a tracking calendar for the all sections of the RFP to include letters of support, grant components, and budgetary items.

3. Ensure that the principal person who will manage the grant is involved in the program design and reviews the budget.

4. Serve as or assign a primary contact with the potential funder. This will ensure that there is no lost or misunderstood information between the funder and the agency. Keep a written log of the questions asked and the answers received, and share them with the grant writing group.

5. Allow enough time in the process to provide a final draft to all involved. This step can help fine-tune the proposal and ensure that you have a great product.

6. Enlist the help of one trusted person to make necessary copies of the proposal. Ensure the proposal has been copied and collated correctly, bound, and mailed. Keep a copy of the mailing receipt. FedEx or another overnight mail delivery system is the recommended way to send the proposal—both for the tracking ability and for the receipts.

7. Establish a protocol for handing off the project once funded. Continue to track reports that are needed for the project for at least the first year to ensure that the project manager is giving timely feedback to the funder as requested. Provide the project manager with a listing of the needed reports, their time-lines, and the contact persons for the project. (This is above and beyond the expectations for most grant writers but it is great for career advancement.)

Writing Style and Format

Although not stated in the RFA, proposals that are written to governmental funding sources and some large foundations require a formal writing style. However, unlike a research paper in which you use footnotes or endnotes to cite references, the references are usually incorporated into the body of the text. For example, one might write, "In 20xx, the birth rate for adolescents ages 15 to 17 in Orange County, California was 38.5 per thousand (Orange County Health Care Agency)." Or, in another example, you may write, "According to a recent study conducted by the Children's Defense Fund (Annual Report, 20xx), latchkey children are at greater risk for stress related disorders." We hypothesize that this style of referencing developed as a practical response to space restrictions, that is, with a limited number of pages in which to present a case, you are likely to resist devoting one to references. In proposals in which there is adequate space, we recommend that you use a standard reference style such as APA and attach references.

Federal and state proposals should be written using a formal writing style that assumes the reviewer of the proposal is a professional in the field who is well educated and experienced in the issues you are writing about. Avoid colloquial words such as *cool, great, kids, guy, amusing, awesome,* and *wonderful,* and clichés such as *loads of* or *at wit's end.* You will be expected to use professional jargon and use it appropriately. In general, you will not use contractions, and you won't write "I said" or "we think." You will need to find the appropriate citations in the literature to substantiate what you are saying. Don't use abbreviated words like *T.V.* or *photo*—spell them out. State your points confidently and offer firm support for your argument.

To demonstrate what me mean by the difference between highly formal and more "comfortable, friendly" writing style, here's a paragraph in which we say the same thing using each type of writing style:

Formal: The sense of community in Nirvana is enhanced through the presence of farmer's markets, greenbelt areas, and ample parking. Each member of the board of supervisor's dedicates one day per week of "face time" at the market place, and the mayor and city council members do likewise.

Less Formal: Nirvana is a comfortable place to live with a weekly farmer's market, easy parking downtown, parks, and plenty of access to local government officials.

Just Wrong: It's lots of fun to live in Nirvana. There's just tons of things to do! You can go to the farmer's market and buy yummy fresh fruits and vegetables, or chat with the mayor and other elected officials.

A proposal prepared for many foundations or corporations may accommodate a more comfortable, friendly writing style. These proposals may be only three to six pages in length. Typically, the proposal is written in a less technical and more journalistic style, as the reader will more likely be an educated "generalist" and not a specialist in the specific field as in the above example. It is recommended that in these proposals, the writer avoid the use of professional jargon as it interferes with the readers' overall understanding of the proposal.

In all cases, the final proposal should be a clean document, free of spelling or grammatical errors. It should be visually pleasing with consistent section headers and typeface of a size and, if you had a choice, a font that is easy to read (think of the reader who has six of these to evaluate!). Charts, tables, graphs, and other illustrations can enhance the impact of the proposal and are now widely used. Avoid using shading or color graphs that do not copy well, as a poor copy will detract from your proposal. (You may be able to insert shaded or color copies into each copy of the proposal in your packet if you think that the funder will not need to make additional copies to distribute to the readers.) Of course, if you uploaded the proposal to the agency portal, you need not worry about making copies for the funder, but do make hard copies of what you submitted for your own agency.

The Components of the Proposal

A proposal is an application tool designed by a funder to gather information from prospective applicants, usually in a competitive process with multiple applicants applying, and resulting in a financial award. The prospective funder can request any variety of information and often asks that it be presented in a particular manner. In a highly competitive environment, the application process and its regulations may be used to ferret out less able and adept proposals, thereby reducing the total applicant pool.

From the applicants' perspective, the proposal is a communication tool, enabling the applicant to express the need of the local community, the value of the proposed services, and the applicant's unique expertise and capability to the funder. A proposal is a multi-layered document, much like the layers of a wedding cake. Each layer has to balance in harmony with the other layers or the entire cake falls over. The same is true of a proposal, since there is often repetition in proposal documents as the writer responds to the multiple questions asked by the funder, and answers are repeated in each layer.

The following sections are included as standard format in most grant proposals:

1. Cover Letter, Title Page, and/or Abstract. These documents introduce the project and agency to the funder. A *cover letter* expresses the agency's confidence in the attached proposal and the outlook of the agency toward a positive response from the funder. A *title page* is usually a form document provided by the funder in the application packet that provides the name of the applicant, contact information, and a brief summary of the proposed project known as an *abstract*. The abstract is often limited to 200–500 characters and is carefully crafted to present the project name, its general scope, and highlights of the project. It can be thought of as a mini press release on the project.

2. A Need Statement (also called the *Problem Statement* or *Case Study*). This is the heart of the proposal, and it describes the community to be served and the problem or need being addressed by the proposal.

3. Project Description. This section describes the project or program submitted for funding under this proposal. The funder will specify how to present the project as to whether it will be established through the creation of goals and objectives or simply through a descriptive process. The funder may provide specific forms for this section such as *scope of work* forms.

4. Evaluation Plan. The funder will want to know how the applicant will measure the success of the project, which is usually presented in the form of an evaluation plan explaining the measurement procedures that will be used to determine if goals and objectives have been met.

5. Budget Request. The budget is developed to include detailed estimates of the expenditures of the project and usually includes a rationale or budget justification that explains why the expenses are needed and how the totals have been calculated.

6. Applicant Capability. In this section, the applicant agency describes its experience in developing and providing services. This section often includes a history of the agency, a description of past project success, agency staffing, agency board of directors, and an organizational chart. Again, if this is a proposal with multiple agencies as applicants, there will be an applicant capability section for each applicant.

7. Future Funding Plans. Many funders are interested in seeing how the applicant can maintain the project into the future perhaps by building in fee collection processes in the current plan or other avenues of income to support beyond this funding contract or grant.

8. Letters of Support. The funder is interested in seeing if other agencies or community members have an interest in seeing this project come to fruition. Letters reflecting community support for the proposed project from program recipients, community leaders, agencies, schools, or religious organizations are obtained and included in the application packet.

9. Memoranda of Understanding. If the proposal includes agreements between two or more agencies or organizations, most funders ask to see a written agreement from each of the partners or co-applicant agencies included in this grant application.

10. Appendix Materials. This may include an audited financial statement, insurance documentation, or any other documentation required by the funder.

Using Technology

The Role and Use of Search Engines

Yahoo!, Google, Bing . . . these are but a few of the search engines available on the Internet today. As you enter a few keywords, thousands of references containing those words pop up on the page. Learning to search the Internet for relevant and reliable information requires a willingness to learn the language of search engines as well as the language of classification for the issue you seek information on. For example, you might enter *teen pregnancy* into a search engine only to find limited resources, whereas entering *adolescent pregnancy* yields an abundance of quality references. Experiment with a variety of keywords until you find the most salient information. Search engines usually have information on the page to help you use their search protocol most effectively and are worth reading.

The ability to access thousands of references in a single search will help you to find new treasures in the form of current data or new funding opportunities. We recommend that you create files on your "Favorites" menu to store the address of these websites for your future use—files named, for example, "Funders," "Data on X," and "Research Articles," as it is all too easy to suffer from "information overload" when conducting searches. For a more detailed description of search engines and using the Internet for research, we recommend an excellent book written by Susan Peterson, *The Grantwriter's Internet Companion* (Corwin Press, 2001).

Review of Funders' Websites

No matter what kind of funding you are seeking, one of the best benefits of the Internet today is the ability to go to a funder's website and learn about the funder. You will find information about the type and amount of funding provided, funding priorities, criteria for grant submission, and, in some cases, a listing of current RFPs. Looking at corporate websites will help you to assess the needs of the corporation in relation to their giving. For example, does the corporation appear to fund "highly visible" projects in which there is media attention and a high public profile, or does the company tend to give quietly to the community in which it is located? Does its giving tend toward opportunities to involve its employees through volunteerism? Look for a section on the corporate page to direct you to "Community Giving" or to the corporate foundation for more information about their giving. (If you are unable to find a link to the corporate giving program, use the "Contact Us" link and make an e-mail request for more information.)

While you are at the website, take the time to learn about the corporation or foundation and what it does. How is the business structured? How many facilities does it have? What type of product or service does it offer? Who are its customers? Having a familiarity with the company will help you to better target the proposal and help you to make an in-person presentation to the company if asked.

Assessing Data

As you compile information through the Internet, you will certainly find that some of it appears to be based in scientific fact and some is just opinion. This wealth of information requires a degree of discrimination on your part. Which information is reliable? Is this a reputable source or a homemade website taking this opportunity to promote an opinion? How can you tell the difference? To begin with, you will find that most of the information that is valid and useful to you on domains of well-known non-profit organizations (.org), universities (.edu), and state and federal government offices (.gov).

The following questions will help guide you through the process of identifying a reputable, credible source.

1. Is the article published or not? If it is published, is it in a respected journal? Are there references listed in the article? Do you recognize the author's name or affiliation? There are many opinion articles on the Internet, so beware.

2. Does the site have product advertising and other "pop-up" ads leading you to believe that the information contained on the site is most likely to promote a particular product or viewpoint?

3. Do you recognize the name of the site as a reputable, trustworthy source for information such as the Red Cross, the United Way, or the U.S. Department of Health and Human Services?

4. Are the data referenced on the site attributed to a source? For example, does it tell you where the data come from, such as a study by the Center for Disease Control? If there is no reference as to where the data come from, be suspicious.

5. Does the website have the appearance of a quality site? Is it easy to navigate? Does it look professional? Is there information about the organization or company posted to the site?

Table 2.1 provides some reputable websites to assist you in learning how to identify a quality site.

Table 2.1   A Sample of Reputable Websites

U.S. Department of Education (www .ed.gov)	Centers for Disease Control and Prevention (www.cdc.gov)	National Institue of Mental Health (www.nimh .gov)	National Institute of Health (www .nih.gov
U.S. Department of Health and Human Services (www.hhs .gov)	National Council on the Aging's Benefits CheckUp (www. benefitscheckup .org)	Substance Abuse and Mental Health Services Administration (www.samhsa .gov)	National Alliance on Mental Illness (www.nami .org)

Electronic Submission of the Proposal

Many RFPs are being issued as online documents. Whenever possible, save the entire document to your computer, give it a new working name, and fill it in. Save an extra copy as backup in case you have a problem with the first. Some of these online applications are challenging to navigate, so take some time to click on all the tabs and understand the structure before you begin. Most often, the budget pages of these documents are linked to other pages, so an entry on page 15, for example, may change an entry on page 2. The best strategy we have found is to read the form carefully and put in some test numbers to see how formulas are set and how numbers move around in the proposal before you begin.

Once the proposal is completed, save it again as its original name, print out a hard copy to review, and, if you are satisfied, send it back to the funder. Request an electronic receipt verification through your e-mail software, if possible, or directly from the funder once transmitted.

If you are unable to take the document sent by the funder and "Save As"—in other words, the document must be filled in and filed online as you go—then we recommend that you print out the document first, prepare your answers, and then complete the document. Remember to check spelling! Then be sure to print the document so that you have a hard copy of what was sent, date it, and file.

Chapter Three

Assessing the Organization

Mission-Driven Analysis of the Organization

In most cases, when you receive an RFP, the funder has stated goals and objectives, or a rationale for funding, which articulates the type of outcomes wanted as a result of the funding. The agency/organization, on the other hand, is looking to find funding that matches its mission and current services, and the needs or problems to be addressed. The better the match between the funder's rationale for funding and the agency's mission and programs, the more likely the project will be funded and that it will be a successful project.

The first place a grant writer will look to begin to build an understanding of an agency is at its mission statement. Every agency's purpose is expressed in a mission or purpose statement that guides the agency through program development and community services planning. Usually, the mission statement is fairly broad or global in nature, identifying the major issue the agency focuses on and a basic philosophy of how the agency is to address it. A mission statement may be so broad as to state, "To eliminate child abuse." Of course, we know that one agency cannot possibly accomplish this on its own; however, the statement tells everyone that eliminating child abuse is what the agency is all about and that the programs it creates will contribute to this end. The agency might develop parenting programs, provide a public information campaign to prevent shaken baby syndrome, provide educational programs in the schools to help identify children in abusive situations, or offer hundreds of other programs within the context of its mission. The mission statement may be dynamic, changing over time to adapt to emerging needs in the community. The mission or purpose statement is developed by the board of directors of the agency (in voluntary agencies) or by other governing bodies (in public agencies) who create policy statements framing the agency's scope and its general approach to the broad problem. It answers the question, "Why do we exist?"

Most agencies have paid staff who translate the governing body's (e.g., board of directors) vision into viable programs that accomplish the agency's mission. The vision statement sets the direction and broadly establishes what is to be achieved. In the case of a non-profit agency, the executive director is responsible for developing the agency's services and implementing them in the community. The executive director is also the link between the board and the staff; therefore, it is vitally important that he/she work closely with the individual preparing the proposal to assure that it is aligned with the organization's mission and vision.

Organizational Capacity

Reviewing the agency's purpose, its past and current programs, and its future directions is a useful process. The following "Survey of the Agency" provides a format for examining the agency, knowing what currently exists in the agency, and assessing agency strengths and weaknesses. The information you will obtain through this process will help you to screen requests for proposals to determine the proper fit with the organization as well as to develop a proposal that will move the agency forward with consistency and balance.

Survey of the Organization

1. Obtain information about the history and mission statement of the agency.

2. What is the service area of the agency (geographic area it serves)?

3. What population(s) does the agency serve?

4. What are the current programs the agency offers?

5. What are the educational background/skill sets of staff members?

6. Where does the agency see itself five years from now? Are there plans to open up new program/service areas, or will the focus continue the same?

7. Will the new program require new competency levels for staff? If yes, is there anyone on the staff who has the knowledge and expertise to manage the new program?

8. Will this new program enhance other program offerings and meet emerging needs in the community?

9. Does the agency have the infrastructure (administrative and financial) to manage this proposed program, or will it need to develop new infrastructure?

10. Does the agency have partnerships with other agencies as well as political support to create and grow new services?

Once you have completed this survey, you will have a better understanding of your agency and will be able to use this analysis to develop a new or expanded program that provides services in a realistic and manageable manner. Agencies are at various levels of sophistication within their focus areas, and your proposal must demonstrate an ability to reach a new level of service. Agencies, like any business, can over-reach and develop too many products or too many activities that are not effective or sustainable. Too much diversity is a strain that can lead to system overload and program failure.

Consider the following example:

An agency has been providing educational programs to youths in schools and now wants to develop afterschool programs for teens. The agency realizes that it does not have community contacts with youth–serving providers and is therefore missing a major link needed to advertise and obtain participants for the new program. It does not have sufficient space to mount the program; therefore, the agency does not pursue the grant. On the other hand, to address this shortcoming, the proposal may include a process to create these linkages and allow for the development of this new network with the resources needed for the program to be successful.

The Agency Capability Statement

Almost all proposals require an agency capability statement. In this statement, the agency presents its history and qualifications to the funder. Now that you understand the history and mission of the agency, as well as some of its program offerings of the present and past, it is a good time to start writing the applicant capability statement. Of course, you will need to fine-tune this statement once the entire proposal is completed to ensure that you have highlighted the appropriate agency experience and described the current proposal accurately.

The agency capability statement establishes an organization's credibility to successfully undertake the project. It indicates who is applying for the grant, what qualifies an agency to conduct the project, and what resources (e.g., organizational, community) are available to support the effort. This section helps to generate confidence that the agency is programmatically competent and qualified to address the need/problem, and is fiscally sound and responsible.

In developing this section, the grant writer must reflect the agency's image of itself as well as the constituency's image of it. This includes describing the organization's unique contributions to those it serves and capturing the community's regard for these contributions. When preparing this section, one should provide quantitative evidence of the agency's accomplishments. A recurring weakness in capability statements is observed when the agency makes qualitative assessments of the organization without some corroborating data to support the claims.

A capability statement should accomplish two things: (1) It should describe the agency's characteristics and its track record, and (2) it should demonstrate how those qualities qualify it to undertake the proposed project. Many times, grant writers accomplish the first task but leave it up to the reviewers to infer the latter. They often fail to present a cogent argument that connects what they have done with what they are now proposing to do.

When writing this section, avoid overusing the words *we* and *our*. It is appropriate to refer to the name of the agency or simply write *the agency* throughout the text. Write as if you are developing a public relations article for a national newsletter, informing the reader, making it interesting, but brief.

When you are serving as a lead agency for a collaborative effort, highlight your agency's experience and also include subsections for each of the other agencies involved. It is customary to ask any participating agencies to write their own capability sections to include in the proposal. A typical agency capability statement will reflect much of the following information:

1. Mission of the Agency—the overall philosophy and aims of the organization.

2. History of the Agency—a brief overview of when, why, and how the agency started, and whether its focus has changed over time.

3. Organizational Resources—a description of the agency's funding track record and of the human and material resources available to this project. (Include the pertinent background of staff, especially expertise in areas related to the need/problem, other professionals associated with the agency, and any special equipment, materials, and services that can support the proposed project.)

4. Community Recognition and Support—an indication of how the agency is regarded, including awards, accreditation's, and honors bestowed on it and the staff, as well as how the community is involved in the agency's operation and structure (e.g., through membership, in programs, on committees, and on boards).

5. Interagency Collaboration and Linkages—a depiction of the linkages and support available from other organizations that can assist with the proposed project, including memberships in local, state, and national networks.

6. Agency Programs—an overview of the unique programmatic contributions the agency makes to its clients and the community, including the aims and types of programs, and a quantitative picture of what is accomplished (e.g., the numbers served, the distribution rate of materials, the cost savings resulting from these services, and program outcomes).

7. Agency Strengths—a description of the organizational characteristics that make the agency particularly suited to implement the project. In general, you indicate what is being proposed and how that fits with what the organization already has accomplished. For example, the agency may already be serving the target group, or addressing the need/problem, or using a particular technique or strategy that it now wishes to modify or implement in a different manner.

Sample Applicant Capability Statement

The nationally recognized and regionally acclaimed Boys and Girls Club of Nirvana has provided 38 years of services to youth in the greater Nirvana area. The mission of the agency is to "improve the physical well-being and quality of life of boys and girls living in Nirvana." The agency's staff of 15 youth workers, seven area managers, and executive director have offered programs to over 1,200 youth per year. In addition, the agency has over 40 volunteer tutors who provide at least five hours a week each of service to the youth.

Boys and Girls Club of Nirvana partners with several other community youth-serving organizations: the LookOut, Okay to Learn School, and Happy Kickers link with the agency to expand and enhance program offerings. The current programs offered by the agency include afterschool tutoring, physical education programs, and nutrition programs that help youth to overcome the impact of poverty on their lives. Program outcomes indicate that 89% of the youth in the agency's programs have improved their grades by at least one full grade level, and 92% have improved their overall fitness ranking by one full level after participating in the program. These outstanding results help guarantee the youth will progress satisfactorily through school and be prepared for a healthy future.

The proposed program targets extremely high-risk youth and mobilizes services for them and their parents. The project will provide 100 families with increased nutritional support through donations from X Grocery Store distributed by the agency, tutoring services five days a week, and a family ombudsman who makes weekly visits to assist the family to obtain needed services.

The Boys and Girls Club of Nirvana is prepared to conscientiously address the multiple problems faced by needy families in Nirvana and have received the prestigious County of Nirvana Supervisor's Award, the State of Nirvana's Youth Angel Award, and the National Best Boys and Girls Club Award. Program staff have the expertise and experience to build the required relationships with youth and their families. One of the parents served says, "Boys and Girls Club of Nirvana has helped my children learn. They get better grades at school now. They help me feel more comfortable to talk to the teachers. I am happy they are here!"

Working with a Collaborative

The term *collaborative* refers to cooperative partnerships and liaisons for service delivery. In the past, agencies provided a set of services to their identified client base, usually across large geographical areas. While these services were vital and necessary, they often were not sufficient to fully address the problem or meet the complex needs of the client. Furthermore, with agencies working in relative isolation from one another, it was difficult to know what services were being provided and the costs of these services in total. Thus, the collaborative service model was born out of the community's need for (1) better coordinated and efficient services, (2) addressing multiple and complex problems, (3) cost-effective services, and (4) more easily accessible services.

Beginning in the 1990s and continuing today, mergers became common in both the public and private sectors in an effort to bring escalating costs under control and to add "value" to products and services. Many non-profit agencies either closed their doors during this difficult time or merged with other agencies. Agencies and funders began to look for new ways to deliver services more economically and efficiently, as well as with more accountability for the results of services. It became common to hear funders use the term *outcomes-driven* or state, "It is no longer good enough to do good in our communities. We have limited resources and we need to know what works. And we must work together."

With the federal and state governments releasing more funding to the counties as pass-through funding, most counties have chosen to meet the needs of the public through linkages with both public and private entities. In turn, new partnerships and collaborations have been developed on the local level to meet the needs of clients and funder alike.

In the collaborative model, "communities" are redefined to better reflect actual interactive units of individuals, such as a religious community, a school community, or a particular neighborhood, rather than the broad geographical boundaries used in the past, that is, the X County community or the Major City community. Service "hubs" located within the smaller community are created with an over-arching vision of "one-stop shopping" for program recipients. These hubs are sometimes referred to as *Family Resource Centers.* Agencies bring their services to the Family Resource Center and forge linkages with the community surrounding the center, as reflected in Figure 3.1.

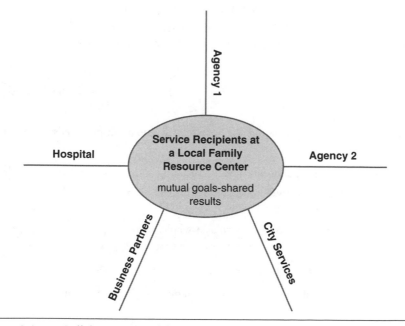

Figure 3.1   Collaborative Model Using a Single Site

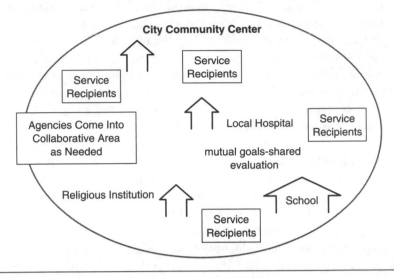

Figure 3.2   Collaborative Model Using Multiple Sites

As you can imagine, collaboratives can be structured in many different ways. The above illustration demonstrates a collaborative serving a large geographic area with services linked to school and community sites. In this case, the client receives services at a neighborhood facility, and the collaborative providers take their services from place to place.

As is the case with service delivery strategies such as collaboration, there are advantages and challenges. The advantages of collaboration include the following:

1. Better knowledge of what services exist in a given area and what services are needed (service gaps)

2. More effectively meeting the interrelated and multiple needs of program recipients

3. More partnering between agencies resulting in new and creative service delivery plans—for example, the nutrition education classes of one agency linked to the parenting education classes of another

4. Evaluation of the collaborative as a whole, providing the opportunity to see what difference multiple services make to a single program recipient

5. Increased access to program recipients

6. Increased ability to track the total amount of financial resources in a given geographic area

7. The development of personal relationships among providers to facilitate referrals

8. Increased participation of program recipient in service delivery planning

9. Increased access to local data (studies conducted by agencies or schools) and shared past proposals to help write the need statement for current proposals

The challenges of collaboration include the following:

1. Significant time spent in planning and at meetings

2. The fact that some funding structures are not yet adapted to fund collaboratives with flexibility

3. Potential problems between agencies regarding service planning and delivery structures

4. Sharing resources and taking shared responsibility for a mutual set of outcomes

5. Cost reimbursement issues if the lead agency is too small to manage the budget

Collaboratives are living partnerships of people and bureaucracies. To be successful, the collaborative must have a shared vision, mutually developed goals, trust in the word of its leadership, a broad representation of collaborative members at the leadership level, and the ability to select and change leadership if necessary. Furthermore, the collaborative involves community members who receive services in important aspects of its functioning. According to Sid Gardner in *Beyond Collaboration to Results* (1999), "A successful collaborative must, almost by definition, have the capacity to tap the energies and resources of the community beyond the budgets of its members."

Writing a Proposal for a Collaborative

When writing a proposal for a collaborative, the grant writer should be intimately involved in all phases of development to facilitate an understanding of the many aspects of the project and capture the richness of the effort. In some cases, the grant writer may be called on to help develop the project and the proposal. One of the present authors led a large collaborative for eight years and has developed a model for conceptualizing proposals in a large group. The following provides a brief summary of the three-part model that can be used by the grant writer to help the collaborative members organize their thoughts and services prior to writing.

Phase 1: Determine the Need and Establish Goals

In this phase, program recipients and service providers define the needs. At a meeting all together or through several smaller meetings, the community and service providers create goals and place needs under the appropriate goal. For example, there may be a need for immunizations and dental care in the community as well as a concern about gang violence. Two goals could be developed: one goal addressing the health and mental health needs of children, and the second addressing community safety. The committee can make as many goals as it chooses or use the goals provided by the funder under which local services can be organized. Once the goals are completed and needs fit underneath, the committee is asked to rank the community needs from most important to address now to less important to address now. (The definition and ranking of needs will help determine the asset allocation to follow.)

Phase 2: Explore Potential Program Offerings and Benefits

In this phase, service providers propose what they want to do to address the needs, indicate which goal area it fits under, identify expected results and benefits, develop a budget, and provide a rationale for using this approach. In other words, are there any data or research to document the effect their approach might have on reducing or eliminating the problem?

Phase 3: Develop the Final Program Concept and the Budget

The program offerings are listed under goal areas. The amount of funding requested is placed alongside each program offering. The column is totaled, and, invariably, the budget needed exceeds the funder's allocation. Using the ranking system developed by the community and service providers, the whole group makes decisions about what stays as proposed, what might be adjusted, and what is eliminated from the proposal.

This process allows true collaboration to occur. In many instances, agencies are able to contribute some services "in-kind," meaning that they will not receive money for these services; rather, they will pay for the services they are tying in to the proposal. (By the way, some funders require a certain percentage of the proposal be in-kind contributions. We will address this issue further in the budget section of this book.) Furthermore, in this model, all agencies are part of the decision-making process, and the "lead" agency of the collaborative serves as a facilitator of the process.

Chapter Four

Generating and Refining Proposal Ideas

The program proposal represents a request for resources to address a need or problem in your community. A strong case must be made as to why this is a problem or need, what has been done previously to address the concern, what will be achieved with the resources requested, how the resources will be used (e.g., services, training), and how success will be measured. The entire proposal rests on the assumption that you have a clear understanding of the nature of the need/problem and have a sound approach or strategy that will have a significant impact in addressing the concerns. This means that your program idea must be rooted in an understanding of the community and the factors that contribute to the need/problem in the first place.

Understanding the Community

Along with assessing the capacity of your agency/organization to achieve the goals and objectives of a new or expanded initiative, it is also imperative that you demonstrate an understanding of the community in which you will be operating. An awareness of the political and social climate; the issues, needs, and problems faced within the community; and the gaps that exist in addressing them are critical to determining the suitability and the nature of your proposed project.

Moreover, the funder will want to know the extent to which you have clarity about the needs of the target populations and their characteristics, and whether you can effectively navigate within the setting to achieve the stated outcomes. Oftentimes, agency/organization directors will "test out" their ideas with their boards or other community contacts as they proceed to conceptualize the needs/problems and shape the proposed project.

Ideas for proposals start with an awareness of the problems or needs you wish to address. Data can be useful for understanding which group(s) have the need(s) or are experiencing the problem and the magnitude of the concern. Simultaneously, you want to discern whether there are impediments or barriers to the participants/community accessing or using the proposed services that should be considered when designing the program strategy. Additionally, the magnitude of the need or problem may be so great, or complex, that a single approach is insufficient; instead, collaboration or partnership among agencies may be the most effective approach to addressing the problem. This section will discuss how data can be used to understand the nature and magnitude of the problem and can provide implications for shaping the design of the proposed project/program.

Analyzing the Community through Data

Have you ever gone without medical or dental care because you couldn't afford it? Have you seen homeless mentally ill persons pushing shopping carts up your city streets? These are examples of community needs because they affect the quality of life of the population in a geographic area, and each geographic area can have very unique needs. Other examples include the incidence of HIV infection, the number of babies born with birth defects, the number of persons who go to bed hungry, the incidence of high school dropouts, domestic violence or date rape, or, perhaps, the quality of air or water. In short, there is a problem in the community that requires attention, and this problem is expressed as a need.

An essential first step in determining the focus of your program is to assess the needs of the community and its resources that can support your efforts in addressing the problem. To document community need (i.e., to show research, demographic data, or other scientific evidence that the problem exists), the grant writer may become involved in conducting research as well as locating various sources of existing data. The following samples of data-collection categories will provide you with a guide to the kind of data useful in both developing programmatic ideas and writing the need statement:

1. Data on the incidence of the need/problem: whether the need has increased, decreased, or remains the same; clients' current physical, emotional, social, or economic status

2. Data depicting the factors contributing to or causing the problem, and data on related problems

3. Data comparing the need in your target area with other cities, counties, your state, and other states

4. Data on the short- or long-term consequences of no intervention (including cost analysis if available)

5. Data on the activities and outcomes of other organizations responding to the same or similar need

6. Data evidencing a demand for service: waiting lists, requests for service, lack of culturally appropriate services, and costs

7. Data from experts in the field, including research studies on effective intervention strategies and evaluation results

The following section identifies sources for the types of data just described.

Client/Community Need Assessment

A needs assessment gathers information about the client's/community's perception of the problem and needs. This type of assessment is usually conducted through interviews with program recipients, through focus groups, or with questionnaires. Many agencies have conducted needs assessments and may be able to share the results with you, such as a local health care council or the United Way. These documents are invaluable to making a case for your project. If you conduct an assessment on your own, it is important to involve members of various ethnic groups (stakeholders) who experience the problem and who will benefit from the proposed program as well as individuals who serve this population. You may find that there are different perspectives on the problem—and thus different solutions.

City, County, and State Demographic Data

Most county governments and universities compile information about the residents in geographic areas based on U.S. Census data conducted every 10 years. These demographic data provide such things as the number of single-parent households, the income level, the number of children, educational levels, and housing density. Some university-based research centers have "geo-mapping" (geographic information systems) capabilities that allow a user to define a geographic area and extract demographic data and other indicators for that region.

Specific problems or issues are often tracked by county government and by state departments working in those issue areas. Teen pregnancy rates, for example, may be found at the County Health Care Agency, or child abuse rates at the County Department of Social Services. Community-based organizations will frequently have data already compiled on certain community problems. The most organized of these agencies will have the incidence of the problem at the local level (city or county), the state level, and the national level. It is frequently necessary to determine how your geographic area's needs compare to other areas.

Journal Articles

There is a rich storehouse of information in scientific journals. You will find research into the causes of problems as well as research on effective solutions to the problems. Often, there are discussions of what are called *evidenced-based practices* that provide data on the outcomes associated with various intervention strategies. Journal articles can help provide the grant writer with the rationale required for a particular program design, with program ideas, and with evaluation strategies. In addition, the bibliographies in the articles in academic journals can help a newcomer to a particular field find other important work quickly. Many journals are now accessible through the Internet.

Local Newspapers

Articles in local newspapers can be another resource to help the grant writer develop a sense of the community's perception of the problem and of local resources. (However, the grant writer must be cautioned not to depend solely on newspaper reports, as their articles are only as accurate as their informants.)

Problem- or Need-Based Program Ideas

Funders look for convincing evidence that your proposed approach will have the intended impact on those identified factors. How does one go about proposing a solution to address the problem or need? Often, one implicitly or explicitly begins with a theoretical framework that emerges from research and practice. Such a framework indicates the underlying causes and posits possible solutions to the problem or need. Using this evidenced-based practice, we draw on cumulative and repeated evidence or data collected by others addressing the same or similar problem. The outcomes achieved suggest the benefits to using particular approaches or practices. These frameworks identify the factors contributing to the problems and how they interrelate depending on certain conditions or client/community characteristics (see Figure 4.1). For example, X Problem (e.g., homelessness) may be associated with Y Factors (e.g., mental illness, unemployment, drug abuse). Social problems tend to be multi-dimensional, and there is rarely a single factor that explains the phenomenon.

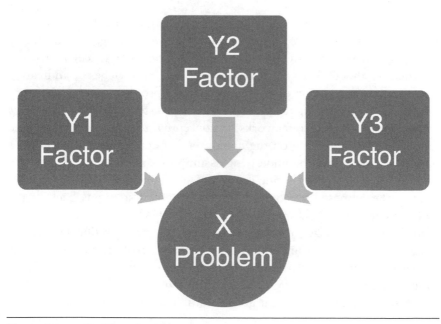

Figure 4.1   Problem Analysis

In defining the problem, Kettner, Moroney, and Martin (2008) state,

> A problem that is inadequately defined is not likely to be solved. Conversely, a problem that is well defined may be dealt with successfully assuming that adequate resources are made available and appropriate services are provided. Still, it must be understood that problem analysis is by nature more an art than a science. (p. 42)

They provide the following questions as a guide to problem analysis (pp. 45–49):

1. What is the nature of the situation or condition?

2. How are the terms being defined?

3. What are the characteristics of those experiencing the condition?

4. What is the scale and distribution of the condition?

5. What social values are being threatened by the existence of the condition?

6. How widely is the condition recognized?

7. Who defines the condition as a problem?

8. What is the etiology of the problem?

9. Are there ethnic and gender considerations?

The theory about how your proposed intervention will address the problem and achieve the desired result is your "theory of change." Your theory of change stems from the research (evidence-based practice) and other information about what you believe are the best approaches to addressing the primary causes or factors contributing to the problem or need. Different approaches to addressing the same problem often stem from different views or different theoretical frameworks. In conceptualizing program ideas, time should be spent reflecting on the outcomes you desire, the reasons for the success achieved, and the underlying assumptions about what you believe are the causes or contributing factors. One should be able to logically connect the proposed outcomes with the proposed solutions back to the underlying causes or factors.

Since it is recognized that there is rarely one precipitating factor, but rather a multiplicity of underlying factors that contribute to the needs or problems, agencies/organizations will often seek integrated solutions. Thus, while an agency may proffer a single solution, it may be that success is not sustainable across different groups until a combination of strategies is used. This points to the benefits of using a collaborative approach, which is discussed in Chapter 3.

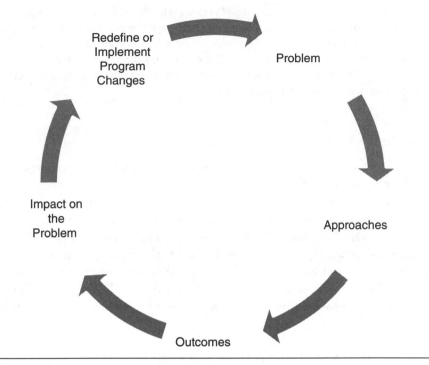

Figure 4.2   Addressing the Problem/Need

Understanding Barriers in Program Design

In addition to the theoretical frameworks that suggest a particular strategy or approach, there are other dimensions to consider when conceptualizing proposal ideas. Key among them is the service delivery model to be used. For example, you may decide that job training will be provided to improve the economic status of single mothers. While evidence-based practice may indicate that this is a critical strategy, the *way* in which you implement the strategy may determine how effective or the level of success attained. There may also be actual or perceived barriers to service that impact a client's willingness or ability to fully engage the service. The following example will illustrate:

> An individual whose quality of life has been impaired by a disease process most often sees improvement once he/she obtains treatment. When, for example, a child is treated for a painful ear infection, the child feels better, the parents are happy their child is well again and the mother is able to return to work, and the teacher may remark that the child is doing so much better in school. These are examples of outcomes that were the result of the medical intervention.

However, there may have been several reasons why the child did not see a doctor sooner to resolve the painful infection: Perhaps the parents were without the financial resources to pay for a visit to the doctor, or maybe they had no transportation to the clinic; perhaps they spoke a language other than English and feared they would not be understood. The reasons why a client does not access service are known as *barriers to service*.

Barriers to Service

Barriers may exist as a result of a client's orientation to services wherein he/she may lack the knowledge, desire, or skills necessary to seek treatment or prevent a problem. An example of this type of barrier exists in drug treatment services when the client denies that he/she has a problem. The client may also hold attitudes or beliefs that are not compatible with the seeking of certain types of services. For example, an individual who uses traditional cultural healers may not value the services offered by Western doctors. Many times, however, barriers are created by the service providers themselves or through the program design, and are usually assessed in five domains:

1. *Availability:* Are services provided in the community, or is the cost prohibitive? Are the hours of operation convenient for the client?

2. *Accessibility:* Can the client get to the site? Does it take special physical needs into consideration such as handicap access? Is there transportation to and from the site? Are there eligibility criteria that may influence accessibility? To what extent are multiple services provided at a convenient single location?

3. *Acceptability:* Are the services in the client's language and sensitive to cultural issues? Is the staff perceived as friendly, professional, competent, and helpful? Is the decor and design of the service setting inviting to and respectful of the client?

4. *Appropriateness:* Is this the right service for the client? Will this service address the problem as the agency expects?

5. *Adequacy:* Is the service sufficient in amount and approach to meet the individual or community's needs? Are services as comprehensive as possible?

Agency Capacity and Sustainability

Another consideration when generating proposal ideas is the agency's capacity to implement the proposed program and to sustain it at the end of the funding cycle. Even if funding is provided for the program, the agency/

organization may not have the ability to fully offer the service proposed, or to continue it after the proposal funding ends. The full cost may not match the amount received, staff training and development may not be sufficient in the areas needed, or there may be a lack of experience in serving the designated population, that is, the service is not within the provider's ability or range of practice. The fundamental question is, "Does the agency have the ability to provide sufficient service to achieve the impact expected within the resources provided?" All of these factors must be analyzed and considered as you explore proposal ideas.

While your immediate goal is to obtain funding for your program or initiative, funders will also request that you address what will happen to the program once they discontinue funding. The typical question is, "Do you plan to continue this project in the future? If so, how do you plan to support or fund it?"

In the majority of cases, the answer to the first question will be "Yes," followed by a brief description of how the program may be developed in the future, what major changes may occur in program format, or what new opportunities may be on the horizon. The answer to the second question may be more problematic for the grant writer. Human nature being what it is, we are more likely to have fixed our minds on obtaining the initial funding for the project rather than concerning ourselves with the funding of the project beyond the current request.

If you view the question from the funder's perspective, you will realize the wisdom of this inquiry about future funding. It is nice to support projects that will do wonderful things over the course of the funding, but rather frustrating to find that they simply cease when your funds are no longer available. From a funder's perspective, it is reasonable to look for projects that have the potential to continue the work into the future.

It is extremely useful to consider ways to "institutionalize" your project, meaning, to imbed it into existing service delivery systems such as schools, hospitals, churches, or other agency services so that it continues forward when you have completed the contract. For example, the state is funding drug-prevention education programs for middle school students. Can you design the program so that it provides direct services and teacher training in year 1, so that a minimum of supportive service and training is required in year 2 when the funding is reduced or ends? This will allow the program to continue on into the future with minimal funding.

Working with a collaborative or in partnership with other organizations can offer excellent opportunities for incorporating aspects of the project across agencies beyond the initial funding. The following discussion will assist you in thinking about the sustainability of your program. Do not be surprised if, again, consideration of this element during the proposal development process impacts or helps to reshape the project and leads you to emphasize certain aspects of the project over others.

Sustainability: Determining Income-Generating Potentials

In reality, most human service programs have the potential to generate some income through the services they provide. However, as many clients are unable to pay the full cost of services rendered, future funding plans often combine the income that can be generated for services and materials with some combination of new grants and contracts. Ask yourself the following questions to ascertain whether the project has the potential to generate some income on its own:

- Can you charge a fee-for-service to your clients?
- Is it possible to market products or materials developed under the project?
- Can you ask your program recipients for a donation?
- How can a collaborative sustain the program through fee structure?

The Life Cycle of a Project

What happens when you forecast the project over a five-year period? This perspective is useful for seeing yet unrecognized potential for the project. Consider the project as having three stages:

1. There is total reliance on public or private funds as you develop and implement the project.

2. You receive some income as a result of implementing a fee-for-service structure, some grant money, and some donated services of both volunteers and product. You are also selling some of the products and materials developed by the project in the first one to two years.

3. By the end of the five years, the project has enough income to enable at least a small-scale program to continue.

Multi-Source Funding

Consider whether, perhaps, there is a way to tie the service into other markets over the course of the funding so as to develop a future for the project. For example, the program you are delivering may also meet the needs of individuals in the workplace. You may develop contracts with corporations over the course of the contract that will maintain services in the future. In other words, you will charge the corporations full fee for the services and be able to use this income to subsidize low-income clients.

There may be some opportunity to seek corporate advertising donations to support your project, especially if the company has an interest in reaching a particular target group. You might include a corporate sponsorship in a newsletter, on materials developed for community use, or on an agency website. The steps you take to ensure the continuance of your project into the future will pay off significantly. As discussed in Chapter 1, agencies will have multiple sources of revenue to support and sustain their programs. Such resource diversification has become critical in the current economic climate, and it is wise that some consideration be given to sustainability as one prepares the proposal. You will want to write the answers to these questions with optimism for the future and creativity. In fact, what you plan for the future may just come true!

Formulating Program Ideas

The previous sections of this chapter helped you to think about developing a program with those to be served foremost in your mind. It also challenged you to look beyond your own ideas about what might be a good program idea and review the scientific and professional practice literature. You have also been advised to consider the capacity of the agency/organization to successfully launch the project and to think of ways in which all or parts of the initiative can be sustained post-funding.

You now need to begin refining your thinking and honing your ideas to formulate the specific direction you are heading in with the proposed program. Similar to a funnel, you start with a number of ideas and directions that could address the need/problem (see Figure 4.3). You consider these in light of current resources, opportunities, agency capacity, as well as constraints, along with any parameters that the funder may have. Ultimately, you develop a program that you believe will achieve the desired results and address the need/problem.

The following steps and the associated questions will provide you a foundation for beginning to prepare the proposal.

Step 1: Understand the need/problem. Answer these questions: What is the problem? Why is this a problem? Who is experiencing the problem? Is it recognized as a problem/need, by whom, and how widespread is it? Are there social/political implications? What factors contribute to the need/problem?

Step 2: Brainstorm solutions. Think creatively and freely about what might be done to address this problem. Dream of what might be possible and effective in creating change and positive results. Examine the scientific and professional practice literature. Consider the strengths and resources within your target population and the community that can be coalesced to achieve positive results.

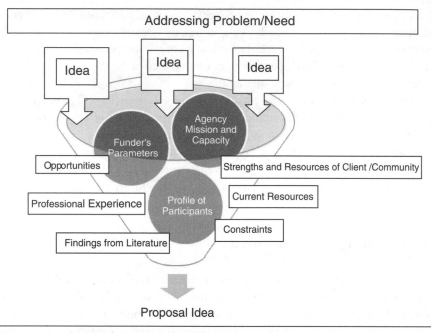

Figure 4.3   Formulating the Proposal Idea

Step 3: Select solutions. Identify the best program ideas from your list that will achieve the desired outcomes. Consider your organization's mission and capacity to undertake the program. What are the strengths and the constraints? How can these be addressed? How can the work be sustained or integrated after the funding ends? Develop a succinct statement of how proposed solutions will lead to the expected outcome.

Step 4: Describe expected results and benefits. What will be the goals and the outcomes from the program recipients' perspective (both short and long term)? How will the community benefit?

Step 5: Think about barriers. What will keep this program from being successful? Is the agency prepared to deliver these services? Are there any broader service delivery barriers, such as regulations related to sharing client information? Can you find a way to solve these problems? Would linkage to other agencies address these barriers?

Step 6: Determine tasks to accomplish solutions. What are the major activities needed to implement the program—for example, contacts to schedule, staffing, curriculum development, site procurement, and so on?

Step 7: Estimate resources needed. What are resources needed in both human and monetary terms? What kinds of skills will be needed to implement this project? What will it cost? What other groups need to be involved? Are resources sufficient to achieve the desired outcomes? What are the community's assets or strengths?

Step 8: Make necessary adjustments to solutions and benefits. Most of the time, we think of programs that cost more than available funding or we find an insurmountable barrier or other problem in implementation. We have to make some adjustments in the project.

Step 9: Identify measurement of outcomes. How will we measure success? What evidence is needed to determine whether we have been successful? (We will address this in greater detail in Chapter 7.)

The following example illustrates how program development, theoretical orientations, and service delivery strategies come together. Let's say that I want to design a teen pregnancy prevention program for young adolescents. I am aware of the fact that this is a developmental period in which peers have a significant influence on each other. In the professional literature, "social learning" theory is one way to examine peer pressure and social norms. I select a curriculum developed on the principles of social learning theory and design my program to include traditional classroom instruction, a teen theater component, a parent-education component to improve parent–child communication, and a community advocacy component to address social norms promulgated through advertising and the media.

Then, as I am reading the program-evaluation literature, I find the types of activities that have been used in the past in such programs, and their success in reaching their goals. Suppose that I learn that the classroom educational component is more effective when provided by college-age adults as compared to teens or older adults and, consequently, I choose to design my educational intervention using college-age students. In this case, I can be said to be following "best practices" in that I am combining a sound theoretical orientation with a proven service delivery plan. I am now most likely to succeed.

Applying the Logic Model

The questions identified in the previous section can now be incorporated into what is referred to as a *logic model*. The logic model is another way of presenting your ideas and integrating the various proposal components. The following defines this tool and process:

> Logic models are a visual method of presenting an idea. They offer a way to describe and share an understanding of relationships among elements necessary to operate a program or change effort. Logic models describe a bounded project or initiative: both what is planned (the doing) and what

results are expected (the getting). They provide a clear roadmap to a specified end. (Knowlton & Phillips, 2009, p. 5)

The basic logic model is derived from systems theory and depicts a sequence of events that are expected to achieve the predictive impact. Using the logic model can help shape the overall proposal and provide confidence that your proposed program or intervention can be successful. Knowlton and Phillips (2009, p. 43) identified components in the program logic model, which fundamentally answers three questions:

"What human and material resources will we have available?"

"What will we do?"

"What will we get from what we did?"

What human and material resources will we have available to conduct the project?

What are the *inputs* or *resources* associated with the project? Examples include

- human resources, for example staff, volunteers, consultants, project clients or participants; and
- material resources, for example facilities, funds, project materials, technology.

What will we do in the project?

What is *the process* or *the set of activities* to be conducted using the human and material resources? What is the overall strategy to be employed? Examples include

- education,
- training,
- counseling,
- physical activities, and
- evaluation and assessment.

What are the *outputs* or *the measurements associated with the activities or services* provided? Examples include

- number and types of participants who attend or complete the program;
- number of hours associated with the activities;
- client logs or other data collected on participants;
- products or materials produced, for example curricula and manuals; and
- perceptions of participants toward activities or services.

What benefit or what will be derived from the project?

What are the *short-term, intermediate*, and *long-term outcomes* or *demonstrated changes* or *benefits* to those who participated in the program? Depending on the length of the program or service and the nature of the intervention, changes may occur at different rates. It may be easier to increase one's knowledge about a subject (short-term outcome) but take longer to *change* behavior (intermediate or long-term outcome). Examples include:

- increased knowledge about healthy foods (short term), and
- reduced Body Mass Index (intermediate or long term).

What is the *long-term impact*? What individual, community, or societal changes occurred? It is assumed that with a successful program, there will be changes that will, over time, have an effect on the overall need/problem. Examples include:

- improved community health indicators, and
- reduction of domestic violence reports.

Knowlton and Phillips (2009, p. 55) argue that to "test" the quality of your logic model, you should apply the SMART principles:

Specific: The model describes clearly and concisely what you plan to do so that one can see the direct connection to the desired outcomes.

Measurable: The ability to evaluate in both quantitative and qualitative means is evident.

Action-oriented: The approach or strategy employed will produce the desired change in knowledge, skill, or behavior.

Realistic: The nature of the project/program is feasible; it can be accomplished under the circumstances that exist.

Timed: There is a specified time associated with undertaking the work and achieving the expected outcomes.

Figure 4.4 depicts a program logic model. The content of this chapter provides you with a framework and foundation needed to begin writing the proposal. The next four chapters are focused on how you organize and write the typical sections required in the RFP. Though the headings or labels may differ by funder, there are standard expectations that you will (1) identify the need or problem; (2) establish your goals, objectives, and the plan for achieving them; (3) measure how successful you were; and (4) identify the resources needed and requested. Let's get started!

Inputs—Resources (Examples)	Process—Activities (Overall Strategy) (Examples)	Outputs—Measurements Associated with the Activities or Services Provided (Examples)	Outcomes—Demonstrated Changes or Benefits (Short Term, Intermediate, Long Term) (Examples)	Long-Term Impact (Individual, Community, or Societal Changes) (Examples)
Human Resources • Staff • Volunteers • Consultants • Clients/participants	• Education • Training • Counseling • Physical activities • Evaluation and assessment	• No. and profile of participants who attend • No. and profile of participants who complete the program • No. of hours associated with the activities • Client logs or other data collected on participants • Products or materials produced, for example, curricula, manuals • Perceptions of participants toward services	• Increased knowledge about healthy foods • Weekly moderate exercise • Reduced Body Mass Index • Lowered Blood Pressure	• Improved community health indicators • Reduction in obesity rate
Material Resources • Facilities • Funds • Project materials • Technology				

Figure 4.4   An Example of the Logic Model

Chapter Five

Writing the Need/Problem Statement

The need or problem statement provides the rationale for the request for funding and uses data and other "objective" measures that substantiate the need for finding a solution to the concern. This chapter will guide you through the process for crafting a need/problem statement.

The term *need statement* is generally used in seeking funding for programs or services, whereas *problem statement* usually applies to research-oriented proposals. In some professions, however, a *need* refers to the lack of access to something that is deemed desirable or fundamental to an individual or community's well-being (e.g., jobs, health care, child care). On the other hand, a *problem* refers to difficulty, trouble, or negative behavior and outcomes (e.g., drug abuse, child abuse, domestic violence). Oftentimes, the terms are used interchangeably and, for our purposes, we use both terms in the chapter. Our primary focus is on proposals written to improve conditions or address a problem existing within your community.

As outlined in Chapter 4, you begin the proposal development process with an understanding of the need or problem as the basis for conceptualizing your proposed program or intervention. Likewise, when you begin writing the proposal, the need statement is typically the first section completed. It provides a convincing case regarding the extent and magnitude of the need or problem in your community, and it is written within the context of those who experience the problem directly or indirectly.

The Goal of the Need Statement

The aim of the need statement is to identify the compelling conditions, problems, or issues that are leading you to propose a plan of action. This section of your proposal does not describe your approach to address the need or problem; rather, it provides a strong rationale for why support should be provided. The need/problem statement is rooted in data and other factual information. The conceptualization of your proposal is guided by an understanding of the needs or problems not only at the level at which you provide services, but also within the larger context of the community, state, or nation.

Too often, this section of the proposal is written solely from the standpoint of the individual agency staff's perspective about the need or problem. Instead, it is helpful to understand that with limited funding available, the funder is seeking to place the need or problem in a broader context and to have the greatest possible impact on addressing the concerns. Consider the following two examples, both seeking to offer a high school equivalency program in the community:

> There are 1,000 individuals in Agency X's service area without a high school diploma, which limits their ability to meet the labor market needs in the area.

> Versus

> X County has one of the lowest high school completion rates in the state and is ranked in the lowest third of counties in the nation. More than 1,000 individuals, or nearly 60% of the residents in the Agency Y's service area, are without a high school diploma. The high school diploma is the minimum required by more than 90% of the jobs advertised. The lack of such severely limits the resident's ability to participate in the labor market opportunities and to be gainfully employed.

While the first example provided accurate information about the concerns in the service area, the second placed the needs of the service area in a broader context of the county and the nation. Thus, the funder can feel that supporting this project has a "rolling effect" by not only benefitting the community but also improving the conditions within the county, the state, and, ultimately, the nation.

An effective need statement does five things:

1. Uses supportive evidence to clearly describe the nature and extent of the need/problem facing those you plan to serve

2. Places the nature and extent of the need/problem in a broader context than the immediate environment or setting

3. Illuminates the factors contributing to the problem or the circumstances creating the need

4. Identifies current gaps in services or programs

5. Where applicable, provides a rationale for the transferability of the "promising approaches" or "best practices" to the population you seek to serve

The need statement makes clear what is occurring that requires prompt attention before conditions worsen, provides an explanation as to why the problem or need exists, and identifies some of the strategies used in other settings, such as evidence-based practices that have the potential for addressing the problem or need in your area. You must thoroughly understand the significance of the need/problem section as it provides the very underpinnings of the remainder of the proposal. As stated before, this section is not the place in the proposal to propose your particular solution or project. Rather, it lays the foundation for your particular solution to emerge as one that is responsive to the need.

The need statement provides an understanding of the impact of the problem not only on those directly affected but also on others, including the community or state and the nation as a whole. A compelling case should be made as to what effect continued *non-intervention* may have on individuals, families, and the community at large. One way to make this case is to contrast the costs of prevention or timely intervention to ongoing costs of not addressing the problem (e.g., effective outcomes-based diversion programs versus incarceration). In addition, there are emotional and psychological costs to consider related to quality of life issues for the program participants and for the community (e.g., impact of being in an abusive home environment on a child's school behavior and learning).

Ideally, the need statement is comprehensive in its treatment of the need/problem, but not boring. Be judicious in your selection of data and use that which most pointedly tells the story of those you intend to serve. (See Chapter 4 for more in-depth discussion on types and categories of data.)

Through the use of data you want to:

- demonstrate that you have a thorough understanding of the need or problem and those you seek to serve;
- demonstrate that you are knowledgeable of the types of interventions that are successful in addressing this need or problem for your client base;
- indicate that you are aware of the multitude of barriers that may hamper the provision of service to this population;
- demonstrate that it is the same issue that the funder wants to address; and
- lay the groundwork to lead the funder to the conclusion that your approach is "client centered" or "community focused" and ultimately is one of the best possible choices to address this problem.

A Guide to Writing the Need Statement

Obviously, you cannot use all of the data you find. Scrutinize it carefully to make the best possible case for your proposal. At this point in the process, many grant writers face the mounds of data in front of them with increasing anxiety. The problem now becomes one of condensing and editing the data to make a powerful statement within a limited number of pages. Drawing on the conceptual framework presented in Chapter 4, this guide now helps you begin to organize the information to begin writing and breaks the need/problem statement into sections. (This is only a template to help you organize and is not meant to be your final version of the document. The examples we are using are based on hypothetical data—in other words, the data we use are for illustrative purposes only, and the funder's guidelines will direct you on what is desired and the length of the section.)

Section One: The Nature and Extent of the Need/Problem

This section could be subtitled, "What is the need/problem and who is experiencing it?" In it, you will try to provide a clear picture of the incidence of the problem (e.g., the number of people per thousand in the population who experience the problem, and the rates by ethnicity, gender, age, and educational level or other pertinent demographics).

In this example, we begin with a factual opening sentence that states the topic and captures the attention of the reader. We begin to define the problem and give a percentage of the total population who experiences homelessness in the geographical area to be served.

The majority of families are only one paycheck away from homelessness and for *(# of people)* in *(your local geographic area)*, this fact is all too real. The majority of homeless (defined as those without semi-permanent or permanent shelter) in *(your county)* are single-mothers with children, representing the fastest-growing segment of the homeless population. These circumstances lead to poor school attendance and childhood health problems.

The next step is to compare the local level data to the state and national data. If the incidence of the problem is greater than the state or national rates, your job is easy, and your next sentence might sound like this: "In fact, in (year), the homelessness rate in (your county) was _____, which exceeded the state rate of ____ and the national rate of _____ in the same year (Source of Data)."

If your rate is lower than the state and national rates, study the data and see if there is a significant change in the rate in your own county from the past, in which case you may be able to say something like this:

Although lower than the state and national rates of ____ and ____, respectively, (your county) has seen a significant increase in homelessness over the past five years and, without intervention, will meet and exceed national rates within the next ___ years (Source of Data).

If your rate is so low as to make your application non-competitive, you may need to find some other very unique reason as to why your community's problem is significant. For example, you may have higher crime rates as a result of homelessness, or more health problems within the homeless population. Contrast the high incidence of the problem to the low incidence of homelessness to make a stronger case.

In this next paragraph, we address the issues of ethnicity, education, and length of time of homelessness:

In (your county), the rate of homelessness by ethnicity is ___% white, ___% Latino, ___%African American, and ___%Asian. The rate for (ethnic group) is proportionately higher than all others. The average educational level for homeless people is ___ years of schooling; however, it is possible that individuals with college degrees are, at some point in time, homeless. The average length of time that individuals are homeless is ___ months.

You will notice that we have not made a highly emotional appeal to the funder but have already put a face on the client in the first paragraph. We feel that the funder, as well as the human service provider, is all too aware of the personal toll these problems bring. Over-dramatizing the problem can work to your disadvantage.

In the above example, the data are effectively presented within the context of the community. When you place data in relationship to other data (e.g., state or national level) or other associated problems, you strengthen your request and increase the sense of urgency. (Note below how effective the word *only* is when using comparative data.) For example, compare the following two statements:

Fifty percent of the young people in the county do not graduate from high school.

Versus

Fifty percent of the young people in the county do not graduate from high school, whereas there is only a 10% dropout rate in the state and 27% nationally.

Section Two: Factors Contributing to the Problem or Conditions

In this section of the proposal, you will address the causes of the problem and the needs of the clients, which may stem from a variety of factors such as:

1. a lack of skill, knowledge, or awareness;

2. debilitating attitudes or harmful values;

3. physical or mental challenges and limitations;

4. dysfunctional or problem behavior;

5. limited resources or access to services;

6. institutional and systemic barriers including fragmented services; and

7. policies, practices, or laws that have negative consequences (either intended or unintended).

You want to account for each of the factors that cause the problem you are addressing. The following paragraph is a beginning to that end:

There are a variety of conditions that may ultimately lead to homelessness. Of the homeless population, ___% have severe and persistent mental illness; ___% have experienced the loss of a job; ___% have recently divorced; and ___% are _____ (Source of Data, Year).

The top reason for job loss in the past year was personal health problems, including depression, followed by poor work performance, a lack of job-related skills, absenteeism, and health problems with other family members. In most cases, homelessness does not happen all at once. The family uses all available resources to maintain housing and often have one to three months of financial struggle before ending up on the streets.

It is also likely that a discussion of barriers to addressing this problem will be included in this section. For example, the stigma associated with homelessness may be so great as to cause people to delay seeking assistance, or the clients themselves may have attitudes or beliefs that prevent them from benefiting from assistance.

Each of these "causes" of the problem as stated in the above example is significant to program planning with different or complementary approaches, and can be further developed along socio-economic and cultural lines, if need be. The second paragraph, which indicates that homelessness "evolves," is laying some of the groundwork necessary to support our project: early intervention to help shore up individuals to prevent impending homelessness—but, of course, we will not say anything about this in this section.

Circular Reasoning

We want to warn you about one of the most common mistakes we see in this section of the proposal, which is known as *circular reasoning* (Kiritz, 1980). Circular reasoning occurs when one argues that the problem is the lack of service that one is proposing. For example, you may write in the need statement, "The problem facing many teens is that they do not have access to a teen peer support group." After writing this, you may proceed merrily on your way to proposing teen support groups in solution to the problem. The statement, however, has failed to identify the needs teens have that can be met through a peer support group (e.g., loneliness, isolation, depression, etc.), and, in fact, gives the idea that the absence of a teen support group is the problem! Consider the way in which the following example might better address the needs:

> An adolescent spends an average of ___ hours per day in contact with other teens in school and afterschool activities. Research indicates that teens obtain approximately ___% of their information on drugs, sexuality, and health-related topics from their peers (Source of Data, Year). From a developmental perspective, teens are moving away from parental and other adult authority and into the development of their own personal authority. In this process, teens attach to and relate best to their peers.

Thus, you have laid the groundwork for understanding the importance of a teen peer support program in addressing the developmental needs of this age group.

Section Three: Impact of the Need/Problem

In this section, you want to look at the impact the problem has on the individual, the person's family, and the community at large, and the benefits to be derived through intervention, treatment, or prevention of the problem. The following paragraphs begin this process:

> The problem of homelessness exacts a significant toll on the homeless person and family. Children who are homeless are often uprooted from their schools and their friends, suffer from poor nutrition, and lack even the most basic of preventive care services. For example, 65% of school-age homeless children are without immunizations. If one is a homeless adult, one has no address or phone number to use to obtain employment.
>
> Once an individual is homeless, the demands on community resources are great. The Government Accounting Office has estimated that it costs taxpayers approximated $35,000 per homeless family per year to provide for the families basic needs. In a study by _____, it was shown that timely intervention targeted at a family in crisis costs approximately $15,000 per year, a savings of over half of the cost of delayed intervention. In addition to the significant financial savings, homeless children suffered less days lost from school, and showed improved health outcomes.

As you might have guessed, we continue to lay the groundwork for our early intervention project in response to the problem of homelessness. We want to show that our proposed project is cost effective and reduces the negative consequences associated with homelessness. HOWEVER, we won't say anything about the proposed project in this section either.

Section Four: Promising Approaches for Improved Results

In this section, you can discuss the theoretical perspectives that have proven to be useful in designing interventions, successful approaches used in other geographic areas, and, more than likely, the barriers to improving the problem.

> Several promising strategies have been developed to address the problem of homelessness. The first is the Homeless Project based in Seattle, Washington. This project targeted a subset of homeless, drug-abusing adults using the psychosocial rehabilitation approach, treatment incentives, and comprehensive services. The program helped over 67% of its participants kick the drug habit, and after a year, 87% of those were employed and paying for their own housing.
>
> Other projects have been extremely successful in helping individuals in crisis avoid homelessness altogether. One project, in Michigan, opened a one-stop service center for struggling families. Through a combination of debt

counseling, psychological services, educational remediation, job training, and health services, a full 90% of clients maintained their homes. In addition, this approach has the advantage of avoiding public resistance to a homeless shelter in the community.

You are referencing the particular theoretical and practical program components that will be effective in addressing the need/problem. This means you will demonstrate an understanding of the applicability of others' efforts in addressing the same or similar problem/need in your area. For example, psychosocial rehabilitation is named a theoretical orientation and service component. It would be useful to briefly describe this approach, giving the success rate, treatment advantages, and cost effectiveness both at your agency and at other agencies. Discuss the pros and cons of particular strategies and consider the unique needs (e.g., cultural, gender, sexual orientation, age, income or educational level, etc.) of your participants.

If a collaborative or coalition approach is planned, identify the advantages of this strategy over a single organizational approach. This chapter also provides a foundation or rationale for the implementation plan or methods section that will be discussed in Chapter 6.

Chapter Six

Writing Goals, Objectives, and Implementation Plan

Understanding the needs or problems in your community and the capacity to address them leads directly to the development of goals, objectives, and a plan of action. This chapter is divided into two sections: Section One will distinguish between goals and objectives and discuss two types of objectives; Section Two will provide guidelines for developing the implementation plan. Together, these two sections describe what is to be achieved and how it will be accomplished. The next chapter will describe evaluation methods for determining whether your objectives were achieved.

Table 6.1 refines the conceptual framework discussed earlier to show the connections among the sections of the proposal and to identify the questions each should answer.

Table 6.1   Conceptual Framework for Writing Goals and Objectives

Determine the Problem/Need
What are the problems/needs?
What are the conditions or circumstances that need to be addressed?
Who experiences or is impacted by them?
What are the factors contributing to their occurrence?

State the Goal(s)
What is the *ultimate* desired result for changing conditions or circumstances?
What are the agreed on issues/needs to be addressed in the long run?

State the Objectives
What will be the *immediate* outcomes, results, or benefits?
What changes are expected during a specified time period that will address the problem/need?

Describe the Implementation Plan
What activities or actions will be taken to lead to the desired results?
What is the "theory of practice" that will achieve the expected outcomes?

Develop a Plan for Measuring the Expected Outcomes
What are the short- and long-term indicators toward achieving the outcomes?
What data will be collected to determine the extent to which the outcomes were achieved?

SECTION ONE: GOALS AND OBJECTIVES

Program Goals

There is often confusion between the use of the terms *goals* and *objectives*, and many times they are used interchangeably. For our purposes, we are distinguishing between them. *Goals* respond to identified needs or problems and are statements of the ultimate mission or purpose of the program or collaborative. They represent an ideal or "hoped for" state of the desired change. They are often described as broad, idealistic, non-measurable statements of well-being. *Objectives*, on the other hand, represent the immediate desired and measurable outcomes or results that are essential for achieving the ultimate goals. They provide more tangible evidence that the desired state was achieved. The goal of a program may be to eliminate child abuse or to prevent domestic violence. The objective may be to improve family functioning by 25% or to decrease by 10% the cases of reported domestic violence in Grant City. Most proposals identify one to three goals. The following are other examples of goals:

Sample Goal 1: To provide a pollution-free environment in the United States of America

Sample Goal 2: All pregnant women in the state of New York shall receive early and adequate prenatal care

Sample Goal 3: To eliminate birth defects in Grant County

As you see in these examples, goals are ambitious statements—they are the desired state of things! As such, they are not generally attainable over the short term, yet they help us to keep our focus and communicate the project clearly to others.

Goals are usually written indicating the geographic area in which the services are to be provided. In writing goals, return to the needs or problems you seek to address and state the major reasons for your work. The following questions can assist you in developing goals:

1. What ideal condition will exist if we eliminate, prevent, or improve the situation?

2. What is the overall, long-term condition desired for our program recipients, for our community?

In some cases, the funders may provide the goals associated with the funding. For example, when applying for funding through federal or state sources, the goals are usually listed in the Request for Proposals (RFP), in which case it is advisable to simply restate those goals adding the geographic area of service. If you are developing both goals and objectives, double-check to be sure that the goals fit within legislative mandates or other funding missions.

Formulating Objectives

Objectives are the *expected* results of the actions taken to attain the goal. They provide the promise of what will be achieved over the course of the funding period. Objectives are specific, achievable, measurable statements about what is going to be accomplished within a certain time frame. (It is also useful to think of objectives as the steps that you will take to reach the goal.) Typically, three to four objectives are derived from each goal and are defined more narrowly since you are predicting that you will accomplish certain things within an agreed-on time period. It is wise to develop objectives for each type of change expected and for each target group. For example, with the goal "To eliminate child abuse and neglect," several objectives may be targeted to parents, one to teachers, and another to the community at large.

When working with a collaborative or a coalition, agencies can develop objectives that are agency specific or shared objectives with the other partners. Developing shared objectives within a collaborative can be especially challenging since organizations must collectively take responsibility for the desired results. (Shared objectives require a certain level of trust between agencies since the objective must be met for reimbursement to occur.)

Types of Objectives

The two major types of objectives, process and outcome, are explained below:

Process Objectives

Process objectives (1) describe the expected improvements in the operations or procedures, (2) quantify the expected change in the usage of services or methods, or (3) identify how much service will be received. Process objectives do not indicate the impact on the program recipients, but rather they are formulated because the activities involved in implementation are important to the overall understanding of how a problem or need gets addressed. They help to provide insight into experimental, unique, and innovative approaches or techniques used in a program. Process objectives are usually designed to increase knowledge about how to improve the delivery of services.

For example, process objectives might be written to measure different types and amounts of staff interaction with clients, to examine outreach activities with difficult-to-reach youth, or to describe interagency collaboration. A process objective focused on coalition building is not necessarily concerned with *what* is accomplished by the coalition, but in *how* the coalition is formed and maintained. Process objectives may be written to study program implementation methodology or to determine whether the program is on track or to address the internal functioning and structure of an organization as in the following objectives:

Sample Objective 1: Ten child abuse prevention support groups will be formed by agency staff within the first six months of the project.

Sample Objective 2: A computerized client-charting system will be developed to track and retrieve 50% of client records by June 30, 20xx.

Both examples focus on the activities required to provide service, rather than the impact of those activities on the clients or participants. Process objectives are not routinely developed in proposals since funders typically focus on giving funds for the direct benefit of the program recipients. In contrast to process objectives, outcome objectives are used to describe the expected benefits to program recipients.

Outcome Objectives

The second and more common type of objective is known as an *outcome objective*. An outcome objective specifies a target group and identifies what will happen to them as a result of the intervention or approach. Outcomes may depict a change in one or more levels, for example, the client, program, agency, systems, cross-systems, or community (Gardner, 1999). Outcomes are usually written to indicate the effectiveness of the approach used by stating what will be different. Changes may occur in multiple areas, such as the following:

- Improved behavior
- Increased skills
- Changed attitudes, values, or beliefs
- Increased knowledge or awareness
- Improved conditions
- Elimination of institutional or systemic barriers
- More effective policies, practices, or laws

Well-stated outcome objectives provide the following:

- A time frame
- The target group

- The number of program recipients
- The expected measurable results or benefits
- The geographic location or service locale (may be stated in the goal, e.g., group home, hospital, jail, neighborhood)

An objective may also identify the target group in terms of age, gender, and ethnicity (if applicable). Objectives use action verbs (to reduce, increase, decrease, promote, or demonstrate) to indicate the expected direction of the change in knowledge, attitude, behavior, skills, or conditions. They define the topic area to be measured (e.g., self-esteem, nutrition, communication) and the date by which the results will be accomplished.

As you develop outcome objectives, think again about the needs of the program recipients and the community. Is the purpose of your program or collaborative to increase knowledge about certain topics so as to affect behavior? Do they have the knowledge, yet still persist in unhealthy behavior leading you to work more directly on attitudes, values, or beliefs? What is it exactly that you hope to change? Will you focus on improving the conditions for a group? The objective should capture the primary purpose of the service you provide.

Many times staff in therapeutic settings have difficulty in formulating measurable outcome objectives and are more apt to develop process objectives. Their difficulty lies in finding ways to conceptualize and make observable the progress of clients, especially those who are in non-behaviorally oriented counseling settings. Thus, staff often find it easier to describe the therapeutic process as an objective, without stating a quantifiable or measurable outcome objective related to the client.

However, as funders focus greater attention on results-based accountability and efficient allocation of resources through such mechanisms as purchase of service contracts, agencies have had to increase their capacity to measure their effectiveness and impact. Having an in-depth understanding of the nature of the need/problem and the factors associated with its occurrence, along with formulating a well-developed "theory of change" that identifies progressive indicators or benchmarks toward the desired change, can help guide the development of outcome objectives. Too often, outcomes are aimed at changing complex or chronic conditions within a short time period and are not rooted in a full understanding of what it will actually take to achieve those desired changes.

Furthermore, an organization's theory of change may not incorporate important factors that contribute to the occurrence of the problem. For example, the goal may be to reduce child abuse and neglect, and the outcome is to improve family functioning by increasing knowledge about effective parenting. At the same time, alcohol and drug abuse may be mediating factors against improved family functioning, which is not being addressed. Thus, "increasing knowledge" may be a necessary component in the theory of change, but it is not sufficient to achieve the stated outcome objective of improved family functioning.

One way organizations address this is to partner with other groups. A progression of outcomes is developed that identifies the change or benefits toward an overall desired end. The United Way of America (1996, p. 32) describes three levels of outcomes:

1. *Initial [short-term] outcomes*—the first benefits or changes participants experience (e.g., changes in knowledge, attitudes, or skills). They are not the end in themselves and may not be especially meaningful in terms of the quality of participants' lives. They are necessary steps toward the desired end and therefore are important indicators of participants' progress toward those ends.

2. *Intermediate outcomes*—they are often the changes in behavior that result from new knowledge, attitudes, or skills.

3. *Longterm outcomes*—the ultimate outcomes a program desires to achieve for its participants. They represent meaningful changes for participants, often in their condition or status.

The following is an example of a short-term outcome objective focused on increased knowledge of the target group:

Two hundred pregnant women living in the Grant neighborhood will increase their knowledge by 40% about prenatal care by June 30, 20xx.

A longer-term outcome could be stated as,

Eighty percent of the pregnant women living in the Grant neighborhood will access prenatal care in the first trimester by June 30, 20xx.

Sometimes so-called *proxy outcomes* are developed. For example, you may wish to improve birth outcomes by decreasing the incidence of low birth-weight babies. However, this may be very difficult to measure. At the same time, research has shown that there is a direct link between women receiving early prenatal care and improved birth outcomes. Therefore, one can use getting women into early prenatal care as a "proxy" measure for the desired outcome of improved birth weight.

In many cases, the program will not only achieve short- and long-term outcomes for the participants, but may also have a long-term impact on the community or society at large. For example, the cumulative effect of women participating in this prenatal program may also lead to an overall improvement in the county's health care indicators.

The beginning grant writer is apt to confuse an objective with an implementation activity. A common error is to write the actual program or service that is going to be offered without indicating its benefits. Such an error would result in the following example of a poor objective:

> One thousand youths between the ages of 12 and 16 will participate in a six-week education program on violence prevention by June 30, 20xx.

In this example, the "six-week education program" is an implementation activity and does not describe what the impact will be on the participants regarding violence prevention. The following questions may help the writer to reach the outcome level of the objective: Why are youths receiving a six-week program? To increase their knowledge or improve their skills? To change behavior? A revised, *well-stated* objective would look like this:

> One thousand youths between the ages of 12 and 16 will increase their knowledge by 40% in conflict resolution and anger management by June 30, 20xx.

As you write your objectives, make sure you are stating the expected *outcome* or changes in the program recipients, and not just identifying the approach being used.

In summary, the following example shows how a single goal can lead to several process and outcome objectives:

Sample Goal 1: To prevent drug use among young people by promoting their academic success and emotional well-being.

Process Objectives

Sample Objective 1: To form a coalition of ten youth-serving agencies to develop a comprehensive plan for providing afterschool activities at two junior high schools by June 30, 20xx.

Sample Objective 2: To establish a multi-lingual teen drug-prevention hotline with a corps of 100 volunteer high school students by June 30, 20xx.

Sample Objective 3: To develop a multi-media drug abuse prevention campaign targeted to junior high school students and their parents by June 30, 20xx.

Outcome Objectives

Sample Objective 4: One hundred at-risk junior high school students will increase their knowledge by 60% about the dangers of drug and alcohol use by June 30, 20xx.

Sample Objective 5: One hundred and twenty five junior high school students who are academically at risk will show a 30% improvement in their reading and math scores by June 30, 20xx.

Sample Objective 6: One hundred and fifty parents will increase their knowledge by 60% in effective communication techniques for teaching their children about decision making, goal setting, and the dangers of drugs by June 30, 20xx.

Sample Objective 7: One hundred parents will increase their involvement with their children's school by 50% by June 30, 20xx.

To recap Section One:

- The **goal statement** provides a general aim and direction for the project, but lacks in specificity as to what will be achieved.
- **Process objectives** identify the approach to be used but do not state what impact it will have on the participants. (It is not necessary for every proposal to have both process and outcome objectives. Process objectives are written when the funder has indicated that desired outcome is to develop a new approach or test out a particular method of service delivery.)
- **Outcome objectives** specify "who" and "how many" are to achieve "what results."

Common errors in writing objectives include (1) putting more than one measurable outcome in the objective and (2) saying much more than is needed in the objective. Keep the objectives simple and clear. While you want to "stretch" as far as possible with a vision for improved conditions or circumstances, objectives should be realistic and not promise more than can be delivered within the time period stated. Remember also that objectives are directly tied to the contractual relationship between the agency and the funder, and as such, the agency may be held accountable if the objective is not met.

SECTION TWO: IMPLEMENTATION PLAN

Developing the Implementation Plan

The implementation plan is the "nuts and bolts" of the proposal; it provides a clear account of what you plan to do, who will do it, and in what time frame the activities will be accomplished. This section is the logical next step after writing the goals and objectives, for whereas the goals and objectives indicate *what* you wish to achieve, the implementation plan explains to the funder *how* the objectives will be achieved. It presents a reasonable and coherent action plan that justifies the resources requested. The design of your program should generate confidence that it reflects sound decision making and is the most feasible approach for addressing the need/problem. This section will assist you in formulating a systematic and step-by-step implementation plan

The program objectives serve as the foundation for developing the implementation plan and lead directly to the tasks and activities to be undertaken. A well-defined plan of action provides the funder with an indication of the reasonableness and rationality for achieving the desired results. The logic model (see Figure 6.1, and discussion in Chapter 4) is useful for capturing the proposal components in a rational presentation and reflecting the relationship among the sections. The proposed funder may or may not request that you use the logic model as a way of presenting your ideas. Nevertheless, it is beneficial for determining whether you have addressed all the necessary elements for a sound program design.

The discussion of the implementation plan will be organized into four parts: (1) defining the preparatory tasks or inputs-resources, (2) identifying the process or specific program-related activities, (3) identifying the outputs or unite of service, and (4) writing the narrative.

Inputs-Resources/Preparatory Activities

Regardless of the type of program you wish to undertake, there are a common set of activities that usually are considered at the beginning of the project. We refer to these as *preparatory activities*, that is, the start-up activities or general tasks necessary to get the program underway. With each task, it is also useful to identify the person responsible for accomplishing the activity and to estimate the time needed for completion. While the type of preparatory activities will vary depending on the nature of your program, the following are typical and are not listed in any time sequence:

- Developing staffing plans
- Selecting site/facilities
- Ordering special equipment
- Selecting or developing program products or materials
- Setting up interagency agreements and collaboration plans
- Building community linkages and partnerships
- Developing outreach strategies and approaches to involving program participants
- Setting up evaluation mechanisms

There will be a variety of activities that must be accomplished to achieve the program outcomes, most of which have resource implications. These resources include personnel (e.g., staff, volunteers, program recipients,

Inputs—Resources (Examples)	Process—Activities (Overall Strategy) (Examples)	Outputs—Measurements Associated with the Activities or Services Provided (Examples)	Outcomes—Demonstrated Changes or Benefits (Short Term, Intermediate, Long Term) (Examples)	Long-Term Impact (Individual, Community, or Societal Changes) (Examples)
Human Resources • Staff • Volunteers • Consultants • Clients/participants Material Resources • Facilities • Funds • Project materials • Technology	• Education • Training • Counseling • Physical activities • Evaluation and assessment	• No. and profile of participants who attend • No. and profile of participants who complete the program • No. of hours associated with the activities • Client logs or other data collected on participants • Products or materials produced, for example, curricula, manuals • Perceptions of participants toward services	• Increased knowledge about healthy foods • Weekly moderate exercise • Reduced Body Mass Index • Lowered blood pressure	• Improved community health indicators • Reduction in obesity rate

Figure 6.1   Program Logic Model

community groups, other organizations); non-personnel (e.g., equipment, facilities, materials, and supplies); and other program-related costs. (One must also be mindful as to whether there are any restrictions or constraints on the program, for example, policies and regulations that would affect how the resources are to be used.)

Process- or Program-Related Activities

In general, we have grouped human services programming into five major broad categories: (1) training or education; (2) information development and dissemination; (3) counseling, self-efficacy, and other support services; (4) provision of resources or changing conditions; and (5) advocacy and systems change. (Note: There may be other sub-categories, but we have chosen to address these major groups.) Remember that program design must be considerate of the diversity within the target population. While there is no single approach to developing the implementation plan, the following questions are designed to assist you in identifying the kinds of activities that might be required to conduct programs in the five major categories. You can use the answers from these questions to forge a coherent and workable plan of action.

Training or Education Programs

Examples: Career-Development Workshop, Job Preparation Training, Parent Education

1. What are the training or educational objectives?

2. What will be the content of the presentation(s)?

3. What strategies or techniques will be most effective with the population, for example, teaching aids and tools?

4. Who will conduct the training? What criteria will be used to select trainers?

5. What will be the typical format and schedule? Does it take into consideration the program participants' needs and schedule?

6. What other arrangements will be needed for the program participants to fully participate?

Information Development and Dissemination

Examples: Ad Campaign for Drug Abuse Prevention, Videotape on AIDS Prevention, Health Care Newsletter, Parent Training Manual, Resource and Referral Service

1. Who is the targeted audience?

2. What will be the content and format?

3. How will it be developed? Who will develop it?

4. Which group(s) will review before distribution to determine effectiveness and appropriateness?

5. What dissemination strategies will be used?

Counseling, Self-Efficacy, and Other Support Services

Examples: Bereavement Counseling, Support Group for Victims of Abuse and Violence, Drug and Alcohol Abuse Counseling, and Crisis Hotline

1. What counseling strategies or techniques will be used?

2. What are the underlying assumptions or evidence of the validity of the techniques with the specific population?

3. What will be the counseling process and format?

4. What issues and content will be addressed?

5. What others resources (e.g., support system, professionals) will be needed by the program participants?

6. What are the plans to reduce the attrition rate?

Provision of Resources or Changing Conditions

Examples: Transportation for the Disabled, Meals Program for Older Americans, Youth Recreation Program, Health Care Screening

1. What resources will be provided?

2. What is the most effective delivery approach for the population?

3. When, where, and how will they be delivered?

4. Who will develop, organize, and deliver them?

5. Any special equipment and/or materials needed? How will these be obtained?

Advocacy and Systems Change

Examples: Legislation to Ban Smoking in Public Places, Education Reform, Health Care Coverage for Low-Income Families, Alcohol and Drug Treatment on Demand

1. What is the research and data on the issues?

2. What are the policies, regulations, or laws that need to be changed?

3. What coalitions or partnerships are necessary to achieve the changes?

4. What are the most effective strategies for effective change? What are important media strategies?

5. What compromises are acceptable?

6. Who will be the spokespersons?

Outputs/Units of Service

In addition to identifying the tasks to be undertaken, one must also identify how much of that activity will be provided. Often referred to as the *output* of your program, this question relates to the volume of work that is expected or the products of your program. It describes the types or amounts of service provided. Examples may include 100 hours of group counseling with 75 drug abuse addicts; 200 health care newsletters printed and distributed to persons 55 years and older; 150 high school drop-outs attending 10 hours of computer training sessions; and so on.

The results or outcomes are influenced by how well the program has been conceptualized and whether there were sufficient units of service to achieve the objective. Compare the two examples of units of service in relation to the outcome of remaining "drug free:"

75 drug addicts received five hours of group counseling.

Versus

75 drug addicts received 100 hours of group counseling.

Thus, both programs are providing group counseling, but they have different determinations as to how many hours are needed to achieve the outcome of remaining drug free. In considering the "units of service," one must often balance the resources available with a realistic understanding of how long it will take to achieve the desired change.

Writing the Project Narrative

This section may also be referred to in the proposal guidelines as the *Project Description*. It brings together your conceptualization of the work plan including the preparatory and program-related activities. Included within this section are subsections sometimes referred to as the *Scope of Work*, the *Methods Section*, or *Program Approach*. Many times, grant writers are unclear as to how to proceed with the writing of this section, as proposal instructions may lack specific details about the content and format. In our experience, if there are incomplete instructions, we then provide a complete explanation of the project . . . starting with the goal of the project, and followed by the objective, the implementation activities, and a detailed description of the evaluation method. This section allows you to bring more detail into the narrative—including the rationale for particular program and staffing levels, for example—than in any other section of the proposal. The following is an abbreviated example of a project narrative:

> The "Learning for Life Project" has two goals. The first is to ensure that all children receive a quality education; the second, to eliminate school dropouts.
>
> The first objective under Goal 1 states:
>
> Objective 1.1: Two hundred (200) low-income school-age children in the XYZ School District will improve their grades one full level by June 30, 20xx.
>
> To accomplish this objective, each of the 200 children will have their educational needs assessed by a learning specialist and be matched with a tutor who has the necessary skills to help the child. In the first month of the project, the Project Directors and the Learning Specialist will select appropriate assessment instruments for the children. Relationships currently exist with the University of Grant State and Grant City College to develop the tutoring pool. Faculty in the School of Education at these universities will assess student abilities, and the tutors will be ready to be matched by the second month of the project. The tutors will spend approximately 100 hours a year with each of their students during the regular school day (see Appendix A: Estimating Time). The evaluation of this objective will be accomplished by assessing student grade point average at the start of tutoring based on their grades of the previous quarter and compared to the grades of the quarter ending after the completion of tutoring. If students demonstrated an improvement in their grades by one full level, the objective will be met. The Project Director will be responsible for overseeing the implementation of the evaluation component.
>
> Objective 1.2: Two hundred (200) parents of children in tutoring will increase their time spent providing homework assistance by 10% by June 30, 20xx.

The writer will continue to address the implementation activities and the evaluation for this objective.

Scope of Work

As stated above, many state agencies require a scope of work form, which provides the basis for the legal contract. It is very similar to the format used for the logic model. This format is useful for conceptualizing the various parts of the project for it shows the relationship between the goal, the objectives, the activities, and staff responsible for the activities; a timeline; and the evaluation. Of course, this is somewhat redundant to the narrative, but it does offer the advantage of a quick, one-page synopsis of each objective, implementation activity (approach), timeline, and evaluation. We have filled out the following scope of work form using the below example (see Table 6.2).

As you study the scope of work form, you will notice that the goal is written across the top of the page and is numbered (e.g., Goal 1). The first column contains an objective that is numbered in sequence relative to the goal for which it applies.

The second column identifies the major activities that will accomplish the particular objective. It is also customary to list underneath each activity the job title of the individual(s) responsible for that activity.

The third column, the timeline column, indicates the start and end date for each activity.

The final column is for the evaluation of the objective, which identifies how each objective will be measured to determine whether it has been achieved.

Table 6.2   Scope of Work Form

Contractor *Geta Grant Agency*
Contract Number_____
Agency Number_____

Scope of Work

County *Grant County*

The contractor shall work toward achieving the following goals and will accomplish the following objectives. This shall be done by performing the specified activities and evaluating the results using the listed methods to focus on process or outcome.

Goal No. _I_ (specify) _To ensure that all children receive a quality education_

Table 6.2   Continued

Measurable Objective(s)	Implementation Activities	Timeline	Methods of Evaluating Process or Outcome of Objectives
1.1 Two hundred (200) school-age children will improve their grades by 20% by June 30, 20xx	1.1.A. The educational needs of the students will be assessed. (Learning Specialist, Project Director)	7/1/xx to 11/30/xx	1.1. A. Student grade point averages will be obtained for the quarter prior to tutoring and the quarter following the end of tutoring. If a 20% increase in grades is accomplished, the objective will be met. (Project Director, Learning Specialist)
	1.1. B. Assessment instruments for the children will be reviewed and selected for use. (Learning Specialist)	7/1/xx to 8/31/xx	
	1.1. C. Students will be matched with tutors who will spend approximately 100 hours with each. (Project Director)	10/1/xx to 4/30/xx	
	1.1.D. Student grade point records will be obtained for appropriate quarters to conduct evaluation. (Project Director)	10/1/xx to 6/15/xx	

Project Timeline

In addition to describing the project activities, funders typically desire to see a schedule of those activities. A visual display of the action plan provides the reader with a real sense of when different phases of the project will be undertaken. It also helps to generate confidence in your ability to effectively plan and carry out the grant or contract requirements.

There are a variety of techniques that can be used to present the project's timetable. See Table 6.3 for one of the most common forms of a project

Table 6.3   Project Timeline

Geta Grant Agency
Project "Learning for Life" Timeline
Fiscal Year 20xx to 20xx

Objective	Jul	Aug	Sep	Oct	Nov	Dec	Jan	Feb	Mar	Apr	May	Jun
Obj.1.1: 200 school-age children will improve their grades by 20% by June 30, 20xx												
Identify and select assessment protocols	X	X										
Assess students learning needs		X	X	X	X							
Faculty assesses tutors abilities		X	X									
Students and tutors matched			X	X								
Tutoring begins				X	X	X	X	X	X	X		
Pre-tutoring grades collected from school sites			X	X	X	X	X	X	X	X		
Post-tutoring grades collected						X	X	X	X	X	X	X
Evaluation report						X			X			X
Obj. 1.2: 200 parents of children in tutoring will increase their time spent providing homework assistance by 10% by June 30, 20xx												
Continue implementation activities												

timeline, which shows activities in relation to a time dimension. In preparing a project timeline, (1) list the major activities and tasks, (2) estimate the amount of time to be expended on each activity or task, and (3) determine how the activity is spread across a time period. The time period is typically divided into months or quarters, and an activity's begin and end points are depicted with row bars, Xs, or similar markings. Generally, when viewing a timeline, activities are listed in the order in which they will be accomplished (a forward sequence).

By examining the project timeline, one sees which activities are to occur within a particular time frame. It is also beneficial to the project director and the staff for monitoring the completion of tasks. Some funders require quarterly reports, and from the timeline chart, they are able to determine what you plan to accomplish each quarter. It is a good idea to include the preparation of any reports to the funder as an activity on the chart.

If there are few activities, or the project has a relatively short time span, a more condensed version of the timeline format may be used, such as the one found in Table 6.4:

Table 6.4   Condensed Version of Timeline

Geta Grant Agency
Project "Learning for Life" Timeline
Fiscal Year 20xx to 20xx

Activity	Time
Hire Staff	July 1 to July 30
Train Staff	August 1 to September 15
Develop Curriculum	July 1 to September 30
Schedule Workshops	August 15 to September 30
Conduct Workshops	October 1 to May 30
Conduct Evaluation	October 1 to May 30
Prepare Final Report	June 1 to June 25

Chapter Seven

Writing the Evaluation Plan

The evaluation plan provides feedback on how well you accomplished the stated objectives and can direct you toward areas for continuous improvement. The focus of this chapter is to provide you with a general framework for conceptualizing the evaluation of your proposed program and for preparing this section of your proposal.

The Benefits of Evaluation

There are many advantages of having a sound evaluation plan, for it is through the development of effective evaluation strategies that major strides have been made in human service programming. Gone are the days where it was simply sufficient to do "good." Now the need is urgent both to prove that good and necessary things are done (outcome evaluation) and to document how they were done (process evaluation). Moreover, the transferability of best practices is enhanced when there is supportive evidence that indeed the approaches used are related to positive results.

Evaluation research can be used in making assessments about the merit of programs, techniques, and program materials. From a broad view, the results of such research can form the basis of position papers for lawmakers as well as the creation of advocacy groups for certain causes. Within the grant-making process, the benefits of evaluation research and data can be viewed from two perspectives: those of (1) the funder and (2) the organization.

Funder's Perspective

From the perspective of the funder, the results of your evaluation may be used to:

1. determine whether the funds were used appropriately, and whether the objectives, as stated in the proposal, were accomplished;

2. assess if the program's benefits are worth the cost;

3. assist in the development of future funding objectives addressing the same needs/problem; and

4. promote positive public relations through promotion of the benefits derived through their funded projects.

Organization's Perspective

From the perspective of the organization, evaluation has numerous benefits, as it:

1. compels the organization to clarify program objectives so that they are measurable;

2. helps the agency to continually refine its approaches to service;

3. provides feedback on the level of effort and cost required to accomplish the tasks so that adjustments may be made in the future;

4. increases the organization's capacity to meet the need through increased knowledge about those they serve and of effective interventions;

5. assists the organization to communicate benefits of service to the public and, thereby, increase public support; and

6. assists other organizations in program development through the dissemination of results.

Developing an Evaluation Plan

In most human service agencies, evaluation plans are kept fairly simple due to a number of factors including financial concerns, constraints imposed by the program recipients, the environment of the program, and limited staff expertise in evaluation methodology. When the program is part of a collaborative or a coalition, data collection and sharing may be especially challenging. Funders will sometimes provide guidelines on the evaluation design expected, or they may simply state that an assessment of the program's accomplishments is required. Read the Request for Proposal (RFP) or application instructions carefully to ascertain the nature of the evaluation desired.

When you design an evaluation, remember that you are developing a plan to determine whether the stated objectives were achieved. The objectives represent the "promise," and the evaluation provides evidence that the promise was fulfilled. There are several terms associated with types of evaluations—for example, *impact, product, process, outcome, formative,* and *summative evaluations* are just a few. In this chapter, we will briefly describe the features of a process evaluation but focus more directly on developing a plan to measure your outcome results. Increasingly, staff are expected to provide extensive information about the direct benefits of the program to the participants (or the community). Much is being written about outcomes evaluation, results-based accountability, or impact studies. It is essential that time and resources be invested in embedding programs within a results-focused framework.

Using the Logic Model

The logic model should incorporate the elements being measured. In examining Figure 7.1, you see that after having identified the *inputs*, or the resources associated with the project, and the activities to be undertaken, the expected outputs are defined. Knowlton and Phillips (2009) describe *outputs* as "what specific activities will produce or create. They can include the types, levels, and audiences or targets delivered by the program" (p. 37). Oftentimes, the quantification of the outputs can be used as part of a process evaluation—for example, perceptions of participants toward the service or the number of hours associated with the intervention.

On the other hand, outcomes describe the demonstrated changes or benefits to the participants or to the community. The nature of this evaluation differs from that of the process evaluation in which you are examining how something was done versus what the changes were. Process and outcomes evaluations answer a different type of question and, when used in combination, can provide a more complete picture of the manner in which the program was implemented and to what extent the outcomes were achieved. The following sections will provide greater distinction between the two types of evaluation (see Figure 7.1).

Process Evaluation

A process evaluation provides an assessment of the procedures used in conducting the program. A primary goal of this type of evaluation is to gather feedback information during the operation of the program to determine whether changes are warranted. The results can also be incorporated to improve the implementation of a subsequent program with a similar focus.

Process evaluation provides an understanding of how you achieved the results; that is, it describes what happened, how the activities were accomplished, and at what level of effort. Conducting this type of evaluation requires close monitoring of the program and may include

- assessment of participant satisfaction with the program;
- detailed tracking of staff efforts;
- assessment of administrative and programmatic functions and activities; and
- determining program efficiency.

Such an assessment can provide information on the level of staff effort necessary to achieve certain program results, the level of outreach necessary to reach clients, and the level of participant satisfaction with the staff, facilities, or program.

For example, in addition to determining whether there was improvement in family functioning (outcome evaluation), you may also be interested in assessing the effectiveness of different family outreach methods used (process). To undertake this latter evaluation, you would identify the outreach activities that attracted families to your program, such as flyers, public speaking, newspaper articles, directory listings, referral through other agencies, and so on. You

Inputs—Resources (Examples)	Process—Activities (Overall Strategy) (Examples)	Outputs—Measurements Associated with the Activities or Services Provided (Examples)	Outcomes—Demonstrated Changes or Benefits (Short Term, Intermediate, Long Term) (Examples)	Long-Term Impact (Individual, Community, or Societal Changes) (Examples)
Human Resources • Staff • Volunteers • Consultants • Clients/participants Material Resources • Facilities • Funds • Project materials • Technology	• Education • Training • Counseling • Physical activities • Evaluation and assessment	• No. and profile of participants who attend • No. and profile of participants who complete the program • No. of hours associated with the activities • Client logs or other data collected on participants • Products or materials produced, for example, curricula, manuals • Perceptions of participants toward services	• Increased knowledge about healthy foods • Weekly moderate exercise • Reduced Body Mass Index • Lowered Blood pressure	• Improved community health indicators • Reduction in obesity rate

Figure 7.1   The Logic Model

might then survey them to determine which outreach strategies they responded to, as well as measure the level of effort and cost involved with each strategy.

Process evaluation goals may focus on the delivery of a particular service or co-located services of a collaborative, or may assess the entire operation. The following is a sample of the kinds of questions that may be associated with various program objectives that may guide you in formulating a process evaluation:

Training or Education Programs

1. What is content of the training? What are the unique features of the training?

2. How is the training conducted? What procedures, techniques, materials, and products are used? What is the background of the trainer(s)? What costs are associated with the training?

3. What is the background of individuals trained, and which training techniques are most effective with which groups?

4. What are staff's perceptions of the quality of the training? How can it be improved? What level of effort is required to accomplish each facet of the training?

Products/Materials Development

1. What and how are the products/materials developed and tested?

2. How are the products/materials disseminated?

3. How are the products used—how often, by whom, by how many?

4. What are user and staff perceptions about the products/materials?

5. What are the cost savings associated with the products/materials?

Improving Operations or Procedures

1. What is the nature of the improved operations or procedures? How do they contrast with the previous ones?

2. What is the implementation process for the new procedures or operations?

3. How do the new procedures or operations affect service? Contrast cost savings and level of effort between old and new.

Improving Conditions

1. What was the "theory of change," and what was the change process?

2. Which techniques/methods are most effective in contributing to improving the conditions?

3. How does the change process impact agency or collaborative operations including staff roles?

4. What are the cost savings?

Outcome Evaluation

An outcome evaluation determines how well the program achieved its objectives. In contrast with a process evaluation, which answers the question, "How was the result achieved?" an outcome evaluation focuses on asking, "What or how much was achieved? What changes occurred in program participants or community conditions?" Funders are more apt to expect such answers since they are seeking some explanation of what was accomplished with the resources provided. This type of evaluation is sometimes referred to as the "so what" of the program—that is, so what happened, so what was accomplished, so what difference did it make?

An outcome evaluation can range in design from simply being able to state what changes occurred in the program participants that is attributable to the program activities, to developing a complex design that compares the effect on participants of different strategies or techniques. In either of these cases, you are interested in the results of the intervention on the recipients. The following illustrates the conceptual framework for developing a results-based evaluation plan (see Figure 7.2):

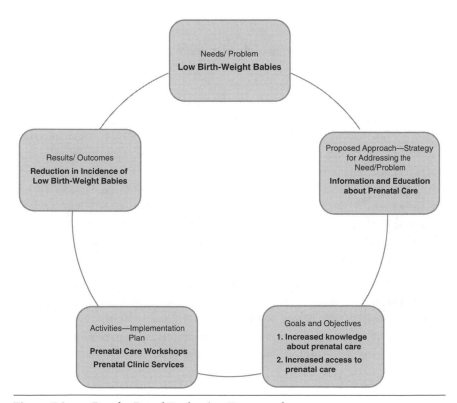

Figure 7.2   Results-Based Evaluation Framework

Four Steps to Preparing the Evaluation Plan

We have identified four steps in preparing an outcome or results-focused evaluation plan. This will assist you in identifying the major components and activities when developing the proposal. Our discussion will intentionally be cursory; for a more in-depth discussion, consult our references.

Step 1: State the Expected Outcomes or Results

Step 2: Determine the Type of Evidence Needed

Step 3: Develop a Data Collection Plan

Step 4: Identify Data Analysis and Reporting Procedures

Step 1: State the Expected Outcomes or Results. As we discussed, your understanding of the symptoms and the causes of the need/problem lead to the development of overarching goals. These goals are translated into measurable outcome objectives that indicate the changes or benefits to the participants. Your implementation plan represents your "theory" about what will work and how it will work to achieve those changes. Having well-constructed and realistic outcome objectives that are tied to reasonable time expectations are key to building a sound evaluation plan.

Step 2: Determine the Type of Evidence Needed. The next step is to identify the evidence that represents the achievement of the outcome objectives. Oftentimes referred to as *indicators*, these are measures used to observe or quantify the outcomes. You should use indicators that are appropriate for the level of outcomes being measured, that is, short-term or initial, intermediate, or long-term outcomes. They must be unambiguous so that one is clearly able to identify whether it fits into the category or not. Terms such as *much improved* or *highly successful* may be part of your outcome objective, but they do not provide enough specificity for measurement. You must define the amount of improvement necessary in measurable terms—how will you know the participants have improved? Will you measure if they have increased their knowledge, will you observe changes in behavior, or will you administer a questionnaire?

Determining the appropriate measures that represent the expected results takes time and a thorough understanding of what changes your approach will yield. When working in partnership with other organizations, it is especially important that there be agreement on the best approaches for determining whether the results were achieved. Questions such as, "How will we know it when we see it?" or "What are the developmental stages toward the ultimate change desired?" or "How can we tell if knowledge, attitudes, behavior, skills, or conditions have changed?" can stimulate your thinking toward developing realistic and specific indicators. In recent years, there have been compilations of indicators typically used in human services programming. The following table provides examples of common indicators.

In these examples, there may be more than one indicator to measure an outcome (see Table 7.1). Additionally, you may be measuring one variable in the short term—for example, did the participants increase their knowledge about a subject? But in the long run, with the passage of time, for the same group you are interested in looking at another variable—for example, did they change behavior or are there different conditions in the community? In an earlier chapter, we also referred to *proxy measures*, which may be used as good representations of a more difficult to measure outcome.

Table 7.1   Sample Indicators

Healthy Births

Increased knowledge about prenatal care

Lower rates of low-birth-weight babies

Higher rates of prenatal care in the first trimester

Reduced Substance Abuse

Increased knowledge about the dangers of alcohol and drug use

Percent of youth in grades 7–12 who consume less than five or more drinks of alcohol on a single occasion in the last 30 days

Improved Parent Functioning

Improved scores on parenting skills pre- and posttests

Increased time spent reading to children

Employs nonviolent techniques of disciplining

Step 3: Develop a Data Collection Plan. Once you know the specific observable measures or the type of data you will use to indicate whether an outcome has been achieved, you must develop a plan for collecting data on the indicators. Be sure to consider cultural factors when developing your data collection strategies. Such factors as cultural response sets, interpretation of the meaning of words, and mistrust or suspicion of how data will be used can affect the reliability of your results. There are several components (see Figure 7.3):

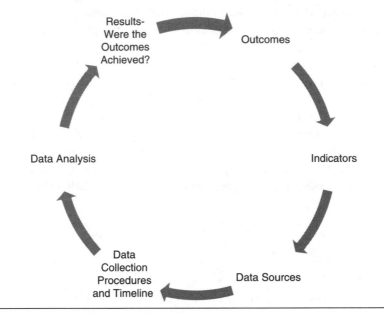

Figure 7.3   Data Collection Plan

When determining the data sources, consider the level of effort and cost involved. Some data may be readily accessible and in a form that you can easily use. In other cases, more effort is needed to retrieve the data. Sources for data include the following:

- Agency records
- Progress reports
- Time allocation records
- Agenda and minutes of meetings
- Activity schedules, agency calendars
- Telephone call slips
- Visitor logs
- Written requests for service or product
- Audio or video types
- Questionnaires, interview notes, program participant survey forms
- Standardized tests
- Staff notes and documentation of role plays, observations
- Service recipient intake and exit interviews
- Community-wide demographic data

In addition to determining the type and source of the data, you must also consider appropriate procedures for collecting the data. (In some instances, it may be more efficient and less costly to select a subset or sample of the participants; refer to a basic statistics book for more detailed discussion on sample selection procedures.) In considering the data collection procedures, one must determine:

1. persons responsible for developing or selecting the data collection tools;

2. how the data will be collected;

3. whether measurements will also be conducted on comparison/control group(s);

4. whether the measurements are culturally competent;

5. human subject protections, including assuring voluntary participation in the evaluation, proper treatment protocols, and protection of client confidentiality, and so on; and

6. sampling plans, including type of sample, and size (if applicable).

Another dimension to weigh is the point in time that you will collect data. These data collection points should also be indicated on the project timeline. When considering the timing of the measurements, think about the benefits of collecting data:

- Before the project—which establishes a baseline (pretest)
- During the project—which monitors progress and reveals interim outcomes
- After the project—when used with baseline data, can show change over time (posttest)
- Follow-up, post-project—determines the long-term benefits

Step 4: Identify Data Analysis and Reporting Procedures. Review the evaluation plan to determine how you will represent the data. Do you want to show frequencies, percentages, rates, comparisons, and so on? Will you compare the outcomes of different subgroups by socio-demographic characteristics—for example, gender, age, ethnicity, income levels—or by the amount of exposure to the project? Which statistical techniques will be most conducive to answering the evaluation questions? Review your evaluation instruments to ensure that you have included all of the variables you may need and an appropriate method to obtain the data so you gain maximum benefit from the effort.

Evaluation data are usually presented to the funder on either a quarterly or semi-annual basis and at the project's end. Unless the funder specifies the reporting requirements, you should decide how you will keep them apprised of the program's activities and accomplishments.

Writing the Evaluation Section

The decisions made about the evaluation design must be incorporated into a coherent presentation. Similar to the project narrative, funders have different expectations and requirements for writing the evaluation plan. Some will desire an elaborate narrative description, while others will request a brief outline or scope of work format. We shall discuss both formats.

Narrative Description

If no specific instructions have been given for preparing this section, the following is a typical format. The decisions made during the conceptualization of the evaluation are now evidenced within this framework:

Outline for an Evaluation Plan

I.   Identify the Evaluation Goals

II.   Describe the Evaluation Design

III.   Identify what will be Measured

IV.   Describe the Data Collection Plan

    A.   The Indicators or Type of Data

    B.   Source of the Data

    C.   Data Collection Procedures

    D.   Timetable

V.   Describe Sampling Plan (if applicable)

VI.   Discuss Data Analysis Techniques

VII. Address Protection of Human Subjects and Cultural Relevancy

VIII. Explain Staffing and Management Plans for the Evaluation

IX.   Identify Reporting Procedures

X.   Show Proposed Budget

Scope of Work

In some instances, the funder will provide forms or require a brief outline of the evaluation plan. Completion of the scope of work form or some similar format may be the only requirement for describing the plans for measuring process and outcomes. This shorter representation generally entails a listing of the (1) objectives, (2) implementation activities, and (3) the types of measurements of outcome/process for each objective.

Other Evaluation Considerations

This chapter assists you in preparing an evaluation plan for the proposal to measure process and outcome objectives. There are other considerations that may not be addressed in the proposal but should be weighed when conducting an evaluation.

In examining what was accomplished (outcome), or how it was achieved (process), one might also need to evaluate the rationale or premise on which the program was implemented. You may find that your initial understanding of the need/problem, your perceptions of the needed solutions, your organization's capacity, or the community's response did not yield the expected result. Your evaluation may call into question the appropriateness of the program's objectives. The objectives may not "fit" within the community, cultural, or organizational context. Such analysis and feedback can help to strengthen subsequent planning and implementation. This can be especially challenging when working as part of a collaborative, for it is difficult to untangle the direct benefits as well as the lack of success of a single organization. It is the cumulative and interactive effect of the approaches used that is being measured. It is imperative that constant monitoring and shared feedback be provided as the program unfolds.

Unless specifically stated as objectives, an evaluation may exclude an assessment of the service delivery process and structure. Yet, unintended benefits or impediments to assessing the service delivery system may result from project strategies and activities. For example, one dimension in identifying the need/problem is to consider potential service barriers, such as availability, accessibility, awareness, acceptability, and appropriateness. Developing an evaluation plan that analyzes whether, and how, the project addressed these factors could reveal serendipitous benefits or unanticipated obstacles.

Reminders

Always be aware that the evaluation can uncover indirect benefits of the project. Such information can be useful in expanding the program and identifying the full benefits of the approach being used. It can also be useful when seeking additional funding support.

As is the case in other phases of the project, there may be constraints on the research design. In human services, many factors go into shaping the final plan, such as a participant's language skills, length of time with the individual, or her/his willingness to participate in the evaluation, even the volunteers' willingness to administer the evaluation. The environment in which the service is provided will also impact on your ability to evaluate it. For example, if you hold a large public meeting and hope to pass out questionnaires, you will find that most people will carry them home with them; whereas if you are in a contained environment such as a classroom, you have better control on the return.

Another constraint on the evaluation is that it does take a great deal of staff time in planning, administering, and evaluating the results; in other words, it costs money. Many times, evaluation is kept simple to keep overall costs down. Ethical considerations can shape the evaluation plan as well. Depending on the type of research you desire, you may need to obtain participants' consent, to deal with issues of confidentiality or anonymity, or to obtain parental consent if asking questions of a minor. Again, it is important to keep individuals' interest foremost in your mind and respect their right to privacy as you design the evaluation. If you are concerned about possible ethical issues in your evaluation, check your library or a local university for research guidelines with human subjects before proceeding.

Most major universities have research departments. It is often possible for non-profit agencies to connect with individuals who have specific expertise in evaluation and solicit their involvement in the project. If you do not have outside professional researcher assistance, be mindful of keeping the evaluation plan within the reach of the expertise of the staff.

The easier it is to implement and analyze the evaluation, the more likely you are to be successful. It is essential that you involve the staff in developing the evaluation plan. Also, feedback from other professionals in direct contact with similar types of participants may reveal variables that you had not considered. Evaluation can be very rewarding for the agency, and ultimately, for those you serve!

Chapter Eight

Creating the Budget

The Budget Context

There is a back-and-forth, give-and-take dance that occurs between the design of the program and the cost of the program. Making the program budget forces the grant writer to think as creatively as possible about how to deliver a meaningful and robust program at a price point that will get funded. It challenges the grant writer to think of cost-efficient ways to deliver services such as using volunteers, obtaining donations from the business community, or charging moderate fees to clients when they can afford to pay them. In the real world, it often takes many attempts to determine how best to structure the program staffing as well as the program "deliverables" to keep costs contained. We have deliberately left the budget preparation to a later chapter of this book, as we believe that programs should be developed fully to best meet community needs and then face the reality of the budget knife. This results in a better program overall even with reductions in service levels, staffing, or operational plans.

As you prepare your proposal, you are thinking of many different activities and services that will require funding to deliver. Even programs that rely heavily on volunteers have hard costs, meaning they need cold, hard cash to pay for something. As the grant writer, it will likely be up to you to pull together a budget for the project. If you are working for an agency, you will need to discuss the proposal with the executive director to see how she/he would like the budget compiled. You will most likely work with the finance director to learn about the project and determine what the direct costs of that project will be. *Direct costs* are those expenditures that are related to the performance of the project in some way—salaries for employees of the project, time of the finance department to manage the cost center of the new project, time of human resources to hire new personnel, time of the agency executive director to supervise the project director and oversee budget expenditures and reports, and operating costs.

The finance director will most likely tell you what the agency indirect cost rate is. The *indirect cost rate* refers to agency overhead costs that are apportioned against all grants and contracts such administrative costs and the cost of agency audits. Some agencies have *negotiated federal rates*, which means that the agency has obtained federal government approval to charge a certain indirect rate on its contracts. If you are preparing a grant application that restricts the amount of indirect costs or flatly refuses these costs, you will need to include the appropriate indirect in your line-item budget. For example, you will calculate what this project's audit requirements will cost and include that as a line-item "audit" under the operating expenditures of the project.

If this proposal and budget are being prepared as part of a class assignment, you might rely on a local newspaper or Internet searches to come up with ballpark salaries for employees, office space rent, and other costs such as cell phone or equipment, and set an indirect rate at the industry average of 10% to 15% just to make life easier for you.

Preparation of a Line-Item Budget

A line-item budget is the most common program budget and provides a budget "line" for each type of expenditure. The upper portion of the budget is for personnel costs, and the lower portion for operating expenditures. The following table presents your first look at a line-item, program budget (see Table 8.1):

Table 8.1   Sample Line-Item Budget

Sample Budget Geta Grant Agency
Parenting Education Project
July 1, 20xx through June 30, 20xx

Personnel	FTE	Monthly Range FTE	Monthly	Yearly
Executive Director	0.1	$7,500-$9,500	$800	$9,600
Project Director	1	4,800-5,500	$4,800	$57,600
Educator	1	3,200-4,200	$3,200	$38,400
Therapist	0.5	3,500-4,500	$2,000	$24,000
Administrative Assistant	0.5	2,800-3,800	$1,400	$16,800
Subtotal Personnel				**$146,400**
Benefits @ 25%				$36,600
Total Personnel				**$183,000**
Operating Expenses				
Communications (Phone/Cell/Email)			$500.00	$6,000
Rent (500 s.f. x 1.50 per s.f.)			$750.00	$9,000
Office supplies			$400.00	$4,800
Travel (at .45/mile)			$277.00	$3,324
Printing			$150.00	$1,800
Vehicle Lease			$300.00	$3,600
Insurance Auto			$50.00	$600
Insurance Liability			$200.00	$2,400
Client Incentives			$150.00	$1,800
Educational Materials			$400.00	$4,800
Furniture			$300.00	$3,600
Equipment Rental (Copier)			$400.00	$4,800
Equipment Purchase			$150.00	$1,800
Subtotal Operating			**$4,027.00**	**$48,324**
Subtotal Project Budget				**$231,324**
Indirect at 15% Total Budget				**$34,699**
Total Budget				**$266,023**

As you study this budget, you may have noticed that there is a column labeled "FTE" in the "Personnel" section of the budget. This stands for "full-time equivalent," meaning 1 FTE = a full-time employee working 40-hour work week. You will notice that the executive director is listed as a direct personnel expenditure, which means that he/she will spend 0.1 FTE of the time directly on this project in some way. (0.1 FTE = 10% of 40 hours, or four hours a week on this project.) The third column is labeled "Monthly Range FTE" and represents the salary range a full-time employee would be paid. As you look at the column and see that the executive director has $800/month of his/her salary paid under this contract, and it represents 10% time, so the ED must make $8,000 a month. The agency has the monthly range for each position it manages on its "Wage and Salary Schedule." You would expect to hire new employees at the lowest end of the range and increase salary over time per the agency schedule. The final column represents a total for the year. (Note: 40 hrs/week x % time = hours/week, and 2,080 hrs/yr x % time = hours/year.) The following table will assist you in calculating FTE:

Table 8.2   Calculating FTE

FTE	Percent Time	Meaning	Hours per Year
1 FTE	100%	40 hours/week	2,080 hours/year
0.8 FTE	80%	32 hours/week	1,664 hours/year
0.5 FTE	50%	20 hours/week	1,040 hours/year
0.25 FTE	25%	10 hours/week	520 hours/year
0.10	10%	4 hours/week	208 hours/year
0.05	5%	2 hours/week	104 hours/year

What Does a Unit of Service Cost?

The cost of a unit of service varies based on the type of service being delivered. Generally speaking, the higher the level of professional involvement in the service delivered, the higher the cost. Medical care delivered by an M.D. costs more than that delivered by a nurse's aide, for example. For our purposes here, we are going to obtain a cost per unit of service to apply a "reasonableness" criteria to the budget—that is, does it seem reasonable to charge this amount per unit of service under our contract? And does it seem to fit within the funder's guidelines? Here's a simple example: The agency is writing a proposal to provide afterschool tutoring to 25 teens for five days a week over the 13-week spring semester. The proposed cost for the project is $50,000. To determine cost per unit of service, we would divide $50,000 by 25 teens to arrive at cost of $2,000 per teen. If we divide this by 13 weeks, the program costs $154 per teen per week, or $30.80 per day. As this agency is providing the teens with access to credentialed teachers, teachers skilled in working with youth with learning disabilities, and a volunteer tutor pool, along with their own workbooks, the price per day is actually less than could be obtained in the community at large. This example meets the reasonableness criteria.

Personnel expenditures are generally the largest percentage of costs of a project. The following are common types of personnel expenditures in program budgets and can be used by you in planning the budget.

What kind of staff do you need to run the project? In almost all cases, there will be some combination of the following staffing configuration:

1. A project director who will have overall administrative responsibility for the project and some direct service responsibilities. This individual has the educational background and experience to manage this type of program. In most cases, funders will look for a full-time person in this role, and the agency will depend on this person to implement the project and follow the budget as approved. The project director will often be responsible to deliver some of the services while managing the project as a whole.

2. The professional staff whose education and expertise anchor the service delivery component of the program. These are the people who deliver the service. Perhaps they will be licensed therapists, counselors, child care providers, credentialed educators, or health care providers.

3. Volunteers may also be used to deliver services. Perhaps the volunteers will be professionals, paraprofessional, students, or general community members. Volunteers provide services under the contract for free. This level of staffing often requires a level of recruitment into the project, a training program to prepare them for the delivery of services (and this training should be included in the program design and costs), and supervision. Using interns or volunteers

Table 8.3   Common Types of Personnel Expenditures

Personnel Costs	
Project Director	Project Professional Staff
Clerical Staff	Student Intern Stipends
Finance Director	Human Resources
Executive Director	Information Technology
Taxes and Employee Benefits	Receptionist

in a project is usually a cost-effective manner to deliver services and contributes to the field as a whole as it builds the capacity of future professionals.

4. Clerical/administrative assistants/receptionists hired to manage phones, paperwork, scheduling, data entry, and other clerical duties for the project.

5. Finance director and accounting staff to establish a cost center for the project, manage the projects finances, pay bills and track expenditures, and prepare financial reports.

6. A percentage of time of the executive director to provide supervision to the project director, interact with the funder to negotiate or implement the contract, and to ensure fiscal and programmatic compliance. Some projects also include a percentage of the executive director's time to attend community meetings or conduct other public relations efforts of the project.

7. Human resources director to recruit open positions of the project, and provide staff training.

As you see in the above example, employee benefits are also included under "Personnel Costs." The agency will determine what is included in this benefits line. At a minimum, this amount will include employer contributions for federal and state governments (e.g., FICA and Federal Withholding taxes, State Disability Insurance, Medicare, and, Social Security contributions). Other employee benefits provided by the employer may also be included on this line and will often include health and dental insurance and retirement funds. The total amount of payroll taxes and benefits provided to the employee is calculated as a percentage of the total salary amount. The benefit amount will vary widely depending on the organization type—many non-profit social service agencies have benefits calculated closer to 20%, whereas government organizations may provide up to 35% or so.

Now let us look at the second section of the budget that addresses operating expenses. Again, it is important to look carefully at the proposal itself and identify all of the items that will cost money. The operating costs listed in Table 8.4 are typical among project proposals.

You will probably notice that we have included consultants in the operating budget and not the personnel budget. In most cases, consultants will be included under operating budgets as a non-employee program expenditure. (We would classify consultants as non-employees as they work independently under a consultant contract, are responsible to carry their own liability insurance and health insurance plans, and pay their own taxes on income they make.) In addition, many state and federal funders have established fixed reimbursement rates for things such as mileage, per diem for travel, and consultants, and you will want to carefully read the Request for Proposal (RFP) for detailed descriptions of what is acceptable. Perhaps other details in the budget will not be apparent until you reach the

Table 8.4   Common Operational Costs

Operating Costs	
Rent	Utilities
Office Supplies	Printing
Equipment	Communications: Phone, Fax, Internet
Mileage	Staff Training
Travel	Project Materials
Furniture	Liability Insurance
Consultants	Advertising

negotiation stage. For example, you might have $5,000 in the budget to purchase a computer and printer, and during the negotiation, the funder tells you that they will not pay for the purchase of equipment but will allow you to rent it; you can then make the necessary adjustments. Read ALL of the instructions the funder gives on preparing the budget. Most funders state their restrictions in their application packages.

Budget Justifications

In addition to writing the line-item budget, many funders want you to provide a detailed narrative on the budget and drill down to what is included on each line and how the totals per line were reached. In a budget justification, each of the lines is explained. The following is an example of a budget justification for the line-item budget presented in Table 8.1:

Table 8.1 Budget Justification for Geta Grant Agency
Personnel

Executive Director: The agency executive director will be responsible for the supervision of the project director, a small part of community networking, attending the funder's yearly conference, and providing overall program fiscal and operational compliance representing four hours a week of her time (.05 FTE), for a total of $9,600 a year.

Project Director: A Project Director will work full-time (100%) on this project with program implementation and evaluation responsibilities, staff and volunteer supervision, and report-writing duties. The project director, who

(Continued)

(Continued)

is also a licensed marriage and family therapist, will also provide 10 hours a week of direct service under this contract. The salary is $57,600 per year.

Educator: An Educator will work full time to conduct educational evaluations, create specialized learning plans, and conduct one-on-one and group educational programs for the duration of the project for a total of $38,400 per year.

Therapist: A part-time (50% time) therapist will work with the most troubled youth and their parents in in-depth conducting sessions at the program site and work in coordination with the child's teacher and probation officer for a total of $24,000.

Administrative Assistant: An administrative assistant will be assigned 50% time on this project to prepare project correspondence, receive phone calls from interested parents, schedule programs, and respond to questions or requests for information at a total of $21,600 per year.

The Subtotal Personnel is $146,400.

Employee benefits have been calculated at 25%, which includes FICA and Federal Withholding, SDI, State Withholding, Medicare, Worker's Compensation, and Health, Vision, and Dental Benefits. The total benefits for this project is $48,960.

Total Personnel Costs are $183,000.

Operating Expenses

- **Communications** has been calculated at $500/month to include $180/month for three land-line phones in the office; $60 per month for three cell phones for the project director, educator, and therapist so that they are available during and after work hours, usage $70; and Internet connection $70 for a total of $6,000/year.
- **Rent** has been calculated at $1.50/square foot times 500 square feet of space for a total of $750 per month times 12 months totaling $9,000. Utilities are included in rent pricing.
- **Office Supplies** are $400/month and include six-part file folders on each participant, notebooks, locking tote boxes to transport files between sites, paper, pens, copier toner, printer ink, desk supplies, phone supplies, and receipt books for a total of $4,800/year.
- **Travel** expenses include mileage to and from school sites, homes, and community meeting places for an estimated 100 miles per staff, or 300 miles per month at 45 cents per mile times 12 months for a total of $1,620/year. Also included in travel is $852 per person, for transportation, and per diem (at State Board of Control rates) to one major conference for two staff members. The total request for travel is $3,324.

(Continued)

- **Printing** is calculated at $150/month to provide worksheets for the youth classroom exercises, announcements for students and parents, the monthly newsletter, and parenting newsletters throughout the year for a yearly total of $1,800.
- **Vehicle lease:** The vehicle (small bus) will be leased for a total of eight trips at $450/trip for a total of $3,600. The vehicle will be used to transport students and faculty on educational field trips. The cost of the vehicle includes insurance and a driver with a Class B license.
- **Insurance** (auto) includes an additional $75 per trip to provide student and faculty health insurance riders and coverage of their belongings for a total of $600/year.
- **Insurance liability:** General liability coverage for the program for all students, staff, volunteers, and guests on the premises at $200/month or $2,400/year.
- **Client incentives** are used to reward students who are climbing the ladder to success. Students will receive back packs, iPods, and educational games for a total of $1,800/year.
- **Educational materials** purchases textbooks, curriculum units for the Educator, and materials that the Therapist needs to work effectively with the children at $400/month for a total of $4,800/year.
- **Furniture** includes desks, bookcases, tables, and chairs at $300/month or a total of $3,600/year.
- **Equipment** rental applies to the copier lease at $400/month. The lease includes copier maintenance quarterly for a total of $4,800/year.
- **Equipment** purchase includes the purchase of three iPads to be used by the Educator, Therapist, and Project Director for a total of $1,500, and one desktop computer at $300 for the Administrative Assistant for a total of $1,800.

Total Operating Costs are $48,324.

- Indirect Costs are charged to this project at 15% of the project total $266,023 at $34,699 to provide reimbursement for administrative overhead for the project.

The Total Budget for this project is $266,023.

Other Types of Budgets

Some foundations and non-profit trusts require a more simplified budget in which you indicate expense categories rather than itemizing line by line. The following budget (Table 8.5) places line-item categories into more general categories. This type of budget provides the agency with much more flexibility in the actual allocation of expenses, and it is usually possible for the agency to transfer funds between lines without contacting the funder.

Table 8.5   Simplified Budget—Foundation or Corporation

Geta Grant Agency Budget Request FY 20xx	
Personnel	
Salaries	$60,000
Benefits at 28%	16,800
Total Personnel	$76,800
Operating Expenses	
Overhead Costs (rent, phone, utilities)	$14,960
Program Expenses (supplies, DVDs, curricula)	4,600
Travel and Conferences	2,580
Subtotal Operating	$22,140
Total Budget Request	$98,940

Matching Funds and In-Kind Budgets

When some of the costs of the project will be assumed by the agency, the agency is said to be contributing this money "in-kind," and this portion of agency-borne expense is indicated in the budget. The funding for in-kind contribution may come from the agency's fundraising efforts, from other funding sources that are devoted to these services, and through its use of volunteers allowing it to reduce costs. It may also be possible to develop in-kind contributions for a specific project by asking participants to contribute financially to the project or by receiving a donation of goods or service that can offset budgeted amounts.

Other funding sources may require that the agency provide "matching funds" of a certain percent of the amount requested. For example, one state office offered to fund 75% of the cost of providing a case management system to pregnant and parenting teens, and required the applicant to provide a 25% match. In both cases, whether "in-kind" or "matching funds," the funder expects that it will receive full credit for the number of clients to be served under the project and that the clients should not be "double counted" for services elsewhere.

The example in Table 8.6 below indicates one way to present an in-kind budget. The first column indicates the funder's portion of the total request, the second column indicates the agency's portion, and the third column indicates the total to be allocated for each item. Note: A similar format

Table 8.6   In-Kind Budget

Geta Grant Agency
Budget Request
July 1, 20xx to June 30, 20xx

Personnel	FTE*	Yearly Salary	Funding Request	Agency In-Kind	Total
Executive Director	.05	$60,000	$2,000	$1,000	$3,000
Project Director	1.0	42,000	38,000	4,000	42,000
Clerical	.50	25,044	12,522	0	12,522
Accounting	.10	48,000	0	4,800	4,800
Subtotal Salaries			$52,522	$9.800	$62,322
Benefits @ 20%			10,504	1,960	12,464
Total Personnel			$63,026	$11,760	$74,786
Operating Expenses					
Rent			4,000	5,360	$9,360
Office Supplies			1,500	300	1,800
Printing			2,200	600	2,800
Equipment Rental and Maintenance			2,800	400	3,200
Telephone			2,000	400	2,400
Travel			2,000	580	2,580
Subtotal Operating Expenses			$14,500	$7,640	$22,140
Total Budget Request			$77,526	$19,400	$976,926

can be used if you are writing a proposal in which the resources are coming from more than one funder. Indicate the source of the funding in each column, followed by a total funding column.

As you may also be interested in applying for federal funding, we have included a copy of the budget used in federal proposals in Table 8.7.

Table 8.7 Federal Proposal Budget Forms

BUDGET INFORMATION - Non-Construction Programs

SECTION A - BUDGET SUMMARY

Grant Program Function or Activity (a)	Catalog of Federal Domestic Assistance Number (b)	Estimated Unobligated Funds		New or Revised Budget		
		Federal (c)	Non-Federal (d)	Federal (e)	Non-Federal (f)	Total (g)
1.		$	$	$	$	$ 0.00
2.						0.00
3.						0.00
4.						0.00
5. Totals		$ 0.00	$ 0.00	$ 0.00	$ 0.00	$ 0.00

SECTION B - BUDGET CATEGORIES

6. Object Class Categories	GRANT PROGRAM, FUNCTION OR ACTIVITY				Total (5)
	(1)	(2)	(3)	(4)	
a. Personnel	$	$	$	$	$ 0.00
b. Fringe Benefits					0.00
c. Travel					0.00
d. Equipment					0.00
e. Supplies					0.00
f. Contractual					0.00
g. Construction					0.00
h. Other					0.00
i. Total Direct Charges (*sum of 6a-6h*)	0.00	0.00	0.00	0.00	0.00
j. Indirect Charges					
k. TOTALS (*sum of 6i and 6j*)	$ 0.00	$ 0.00	$ 0.00	$ 0.00	$ 0.00
7. Program Income	$	$	$	$	$ 0.00

SECTION C - NON-FEDERAL RESOURCES

(a) Grant Program	(b) Applicant	(c) State	(d) Other Sources	(e) TOTALS
8.	$	$	$	0.00
9.				0.00
10.				0.00
11.				0.00
12. TOTAL (sum of lines 8-11)	$ 0.00	$ 0.00	$ 0.00	0.00

SECTION D - FORECASTED CASH NEEDS

	Total for 1st Year	1st Quarter	2nd Quarter	3rd Quarter	4th Quarter
13. Federal	$ 0.00	$	$	$	$
14. Non-Federal	0.00				
15. TOTAL (sum of lines 13 and 14)	$ 0.00	$ 0.00	$ 0.00	$ 0.00	$ 0.00

SECTION E - BUDGET ESTIMATES OF FEDERAL FUNDS NEEDED FOR BALANCE OF THE PROJECT

(a) Grant Program	FUTURE FUNDING PERIODS (Years)			
	(b) First	(c) Second	(d) Third	(e) Fourth
16.	$	$	$	$
17.				
18.				
19.				
20. TOTAL (sum of lines 16-19)	$ 0.00	$ 0.00	$ 0.00	$ 0.00

SECTION F - OTHER BUDGET INFORMATION

21. Direct Charges: 22. Indirect Charges:

23. Remarks:

Source: From "Budget Information: Non-Construction Programs" Standard Form 424-A. Office of Management and Budget, Washington D.C. 20503. http://www.acf.hhs.gov/programs/ofs/grants/sf424a.pdf

Other Budgeting Issues

Budget Adjustment

At times during the contract year, changes may need to be made in the budget. These changes may be due to a desire to reallocate savings in one area to cover overages in another. Some funders will allow for a transfer between line items to a small extent without their approval, but, in most cases, the funder wants to ensure the integrity of the proposed services if there are significant changes in funding. This process of requesting a transfer between lines is called a *budget adjustment.*

As you will see in this adjustment, one column lists the current contract totals for the year, another indicates the amount of money you want to add or subtract from the column, and the final column indicates the new totals. With budget adjustments, you are not changing the total amount that you have to work with, just reallocating the money between lines.

Changes to a budget are most often accepted by the funder on a specific timeline, for example, a funder may only accept adjustments in the last quarter of the contract. Another funder may ask that adjustments be made quarterly, so it is best to talk to your contract officer or other grant contact to learn how best to proceed with budget changes. It is also useful to obtain approval of the proposed changes in advance if possible.

The adjusted budget will most often need to have a written explanation attached, which describes what has happened, on a per line basis, to necessitate the request for a change. In the explanation, you will tell the funder why there is excess money in some lines and the cause of a deficit in others. The funder will be looking for a legitimate rationale to move funds between lines (see Table 8.8 on the next page).

Such a rationale will usually consist of unexpected cost increases in products or materials used by the project; a reduction in the amount of salary and benefits used because of a vacancy in a position resulting in savings in personnel costs; or, changes in the level of intensity in staffing or services provided resulting in increased costs.

Budget Amendment

If, during the course of the contract, your scope of work has been expanded or reduced, you may need to do a budget amendment reflecting this change. A simple way to think about it is this: When you need to shift money and it does not alter the scope of work in any way, you write an adjustment. If something has happened to significantly alter the scope—for

Table 8.8   Budget Adjustment

	Prior Approved Amount	Adjustment Effective 10/1/20xx	New Approved Amount
Personnel			
Executive Director	$2,000	(100)	$1,900
Project Director	38,000	0	38,000
Clerical	12,522	0	12,522
Benefits	10,504	(20)	10,484
Total Personnel	$52,522	(120)	$52,502
Operating Expenses			
Rent	$4,000	0	$4,000
Office Supplies	1,500	500	2,000
Printing	2,200	(380)	1,820
Equipment Rental Maintenance	2,800	(500)	2,300
Telephone	2,000	0	2,000
Travel	2,000	500	2,500
Subtotal Operating	14,500	120	14,500
Total Budget	$77,526	0	$77,526

example, the funder has asked you to take on an additional project or activity and will provide more money—you will write an amendment. Some funders require an amendment if you are seeking to move more than $5,000 (or some other predetermined amount). Amendments are usually written using the same budget format for requesting adjustments.

The major difference between an amendment and an adjustment is that the amendment changes your contract with the funder and goes through a formal approval process. You will receive a new copy of the contract with the amended budget and any program changes resulting from the amendment.

Contract Negotiations

It will be a good day when the agency is notified that the proposal has been approved for funding. If the funding is less than requested, you will most likely reconvene with the team to discuss the changes that will need to be made to the budget and program. As the grant writer, you are in a key position to know how the budget impacts the program and vice versa. Be conscious of the possible "domino effect" that a change in the budget will have on the entire program and develop a couple of possible changes to the proposal that will meet the funders request. Discuss these changes with your team and prepare to (1) attend the contract negotiation session or (2) submit the changes to the funder directly.

If there is a formal contract negotiation, you, and most likely the agency executive director, will meet face-to-face with the funder, review what is going to be provided by the contract, review the changes that reduced funding has made to the proposal, and answer other questions the funder may have. The funder may want to ask questions about the project or make changes to the project. Always approach these negotiations carefully, as it can be very easy to make changes in a project that will be very difficult to live with.

No one knows the project better than you. Approach the negotiations from the perspective of win-win. The funder wants a good program just as you do. Here are a few guidelines for negotiating contracts:

1. Re-read the proposal just prior to going into the negotiations. Be intimately familiar with all of it just as you were when writing it six months ago.

2. Create an atmosphere of partnership with the contract negotiator.

3. Take your time when you make changes. Look at the impact any change will have on the objectives even if this means that you ask for additional time to consider the impact of the requested changes on the project.

4. Be prepared to discuss your rationale for keeping the project as initially developed in the proposal, and don't be too anxious to change it.

5. If the agency has not been awarded the full amount requested, prepare a new version of the proposal in advance of the meeting. This enables you to have time to re-think the budget and program, and decide on the revisions that make the most sense to you.

6. Remember to maintain your integrity. If you know that the agency cannot do the job for the amount of money offered, say so. In this case, the agency will need to decide if it is worth pursuing. It is possible, and we have seen it happen, that the agency will choose to turn down the contract because accepting it would be too costly to the agency.

Subcontracting

Subcontracting means that your agency receives the master contract from the funder. This makes your agency the primary contractor or the "lead agency." The lead agency then prepares subcontracts for the other agency involved in the project. This is a typical arrangement used by a collaborative or by two or more community agencies in partnership. The subcontracting agency is bound by the same contractual terms as the primary contractor. The primary contractor is responsible for ensuring that the subcontracting agency abides by the terms of the contract and usually prepares a legally binding agreement to this effect. (For a more in-depth treatment of the topic of contracts and subcontracting, see Kettner, Moroney, & Martin, 2008.)

If you are using subcontractors, you have to address this issue within the body of the grant itself to clearly identify by objectives the role of the subcontractor in the contract, and to establish the credibility of the subcontractor in the applicant capability section. The budget of the subcontractor is included in the main budget and fully described in the budget justification.

As you review the steps in budget preparation, you can see why this should not be left to the last minute. Preparing the budget requires that you have a thorough grasp of the project, including all of the details of the implementation activities, so that you can be certain not to omit any major costs. REMEMBER: Changes in the program will have an impact on the budget, and changes in the budget will have an impact on the program.

Chapter Nine

Finishing Touches

This chapter provides an overview of what some refer to as the *finishing touches* of the proposal. These are the items that complete the proposal and are often prepared after the other sections have been written. You will want to follow the funder's guidelines regarding what items are requested and acceptable to attach to the proposal in an appendix, and often these include the following:

1. Letters of Support

2. A copy of documents demonstrating agency accomplishments, including awards and recognition from local, state, and national groups

3. A listing of the members of the agency's board of directors and their qualifications and affiliations

4. IRS 501(c) 3 letter

5. Copy of agency financial statements for the current year

6. Copy of agency audited financial statements for the past year

7. Organizational chart

Requesting Letters of Support

Letters of support are usually obtained from other agencies, possible clients, and influential community members including elected officials. It is most usual to make contact with the potential letter writer by phone, explain the project, and ascertain their willingness to write a letter of support. If the response is positive, fax or e-mail a sample letter to them that contains enough details about the project that they can write their letter from it, or, simply copy your letter onto their letterhead and sign it. You will also provide the writer with directions as to when the letter is due and how you want to receive the letter—are you going to pick it up, or have it mailed or faxed to you? Below is a sample of a request for a letter of support:

Sample Letter of Support

Dear Agency Executive Director:

The Geta Grant agency is applying for $100,000 in funding to the Office of Health and Human Services to fund a case management system for the Families First Collaborative. This project, called "Management for Health," provides a full-time case worker to address the mental health, educational, parenting, employment, housing, food, and health needs of the highest-risk Latino and white families in the cities of Lemon, Tangerine, and Banana. We expect that over 200 families with multiple needs will be served in the first year. In addition, our project will evaluate the effectiveness of case management on health and mental health outcomes with this population.

Agencies included in this collaborative proposal include the Department of Education, A Fine Health Center, the Metal Health Center, the Human Interaction Commission, Housing First, and the Food Bank Distribution Center.

If you see the need for these services in our community, or if you are willing to partner with us in this proposal to provide X, Y, and Z, please write a letter of support addressed to: Mary Smith, Program Officer, Office of Health and Human Services, Department 007, 200 State Lane, Room 123, Our Town, CA 90009 *but send the letter* to me: Grant writer, Geta Grant Agency, 1111 One Street, This Town, CA 90002. We thank you for your support. Please call us to pick up the letter by Friday, June 2, 20xx.

As the grant writer, be prepared to make follow-up phone calls to the agencies and to pick up the letter if you are nearing the proposal deadline. It is wise to request the letters early, as you are preparing the other sections of the proposal, to avoid the delay as the proposal deadline approaches. In some instances, you may be asked by the organizations to draft a letter of support for them. This is often ideal as you can be very specific about the items you want emphasized by each supporting source.

Proposal Abstract

The abstract is usually written after the other sections, since it gives an overview of the entire project. Unless the funder provides other instructions or forms, the abstract is typically no longer than one page. The abstract is used by the funder to screen the proposal for appropriateness in light of their funding objectives. A glance at the abstract also assists staff in disseminating the document to the proper review committees or funding offices. Once a proposal is funded, the abstract is often used by funders to convey to the public their funding decisions and activities.

Although it is sometimes hurriedly written at the end, care and attention should be given to its content. This is *not* the proposal introduction; rather, it is a complete summary of the entire project. As such, the abstract should parallel the major sections of the proposal. An abstract will typically

1. identify the agency requesting the funds;

2. describe the target population;

3. summarize the need/problem statement highlighting data that show the magnitude, or extent, of the problem;

4. provide a synopsis of the project objectives including goals and objectives;

5. highlight the evaluation plan and the expected outcomes or results of the project; and

6. provide an "amount requested" figure.

A Sample Abstract

The Management for Health project will serve over 200 low-income Latino parents and help them to connect to vital services in housing, food, employment, mental health, physical health, and parenting. Bringing the expertise and talents of the Geta Grant Agency as lead agency along with the Department of Education, A Fine Health Center, the Mental Health Center, the Human Interaction Commission, Housing First, and the Food Bank Distribution Center, this project uses a Case Manager/Consultant to work with the parents one on one and immediately link the parent to appropriate, waiting services. We expect this project with its requested budget of $100,000 to improve the health of all of the family members, and increase family emotional and financial stability.

Title and Title Page

Develop a title that reflects the major goal(s) of the project. While one may develop a "catchy" title, its meaning should be readily understood by the reviewers. A descriptive subtitle might be used to clarify. Avoid long titles, or ones that are used too often by other projects.

A title page usually accompanies the proposal. Federal and state agencies will often provide the face sheets necessary. While there is no standard format for the title page, the following is typical:

The Project Title

The Name of the Agency Submitting Grant

Agency Address

Name of Prospective Funder

Project Begin and End Dates

Amount Requested

Cover Letter

A letter of transmittal on agency stationery, signed by the appropriate organizational official, should be prepared. The letter conveys interest in the funder's mandate and mission, and states how the project fits within these mandates. The letter should be brief (usually one page). It should indicate the agency's board approval of the proposal; the contact person, with telephone number; the amount requested; and the willingness to respond to any questions about the project. Also include a paragraph that summarizes the project as well.

Remember that the letter is often the first contact between the agency requesting funds and the prospective funder. Set a tone of professionalism and competency. The letter should be written on agency letterhead.

A Sample Cover Letter

Dear Mr./Ms. Funding Officer:

The Geta Grant Agency, serving as lead agency for this project, enthusiastically submits this proposal "Management for Health" in response to your RFP titled "Community Funding Initiatives." This exciting collaborative partnership will provide direct case management linkage bringing vital services for the Latino community: housing, food, employment, mental health, physical health, and parenting. For the first time in county history, parents will have an advocate and mentor to guide them through a system of services and allow them to deal holistically with problems. The project will lead to improved health outcomes for all family members as well as increased family emotional and financial stability. Each of these variables will be measured in an outcome study associated with the project.

The partners in this collaborative include: the Department of Education, A Fine Health Center, the Mental Health Center, the Human Interaction Commission, Housing First, and the Food Bank Distribution Center. As you will see in the proposal, each of the partners brings a wealth of services and expertise to the target population of 200 low-income Latino parents, and each partner is committed to create success. A series of educational programs will be offered to the community, health clinics will be offered via mobile van weekly at key locations, parents will receive information and linkage to services immediately accessible to them, and transportation needs will be met. There has never been a more thorough project to meet these needs in the history of the county. Outcome evaluation on this project will measure success in all key areas.

We are available to respond to any questions you may have about this proposal. Please contact me at (888) 888-8888.

Sincerely,

Executive Director or President, Board of Directors

You will want to present the funder with the final package in the format requested. If the funder asks for a certain number of copies, or for the proposal to be bound in a certain manner (e.g., stapled in the upper-left corner), you should comply with the guidelines. Be certain to leave enough time to review the final package after it has been copied and collated—this is a tedious task and requires an attention to detail so pages do not get out of order. Once your packet is complete, do the "dance of joy," and send it on its way to bring resources to those you serve in the community. We wish you many successful grants!

Appendix A

Estimating Time

In this section, we have provided for the beginning grant writer an illustration of the process involved in calculating a staff person's time expenditure on a project. Let's suppose that Geta Clinic wants to provide an AIDS-prevention education program in the county schools. The objective states:

Three thousand (3,000) at-risk youth will increase their knowledge by 30% on HIV transmission and risk-reduction behaviors by June 30, 20xx.

The implementation activities, with staff responsibilities include the following:

1. Relationship established with schools (Project Director, Community Educator)

2. Education programs developed and scheduled (Community Educator, Administrative Assistant)

3. Parent Orientation Nights planned and conducted (Community Educator)

4. Two 1-hour educational presentations provided in the student's regular classroom on the nature of HIV transmission, risky behaviors, decision-making skills, and assertiveness training (Community Educator)

5. Student evaluation using pre- and posttest to indicate knowledge change (Community Educator and Administrative Assistant)

Someone without any knowledge about community education might say,

Okay, this is simple. An average class size would be 25. Divide 3,000 youths by 25 per class to find out how many actual classes you need; that equals 120 classes. Since the educator will spend two hours in each class, that is a total of 240 teaching hours. If I divide 240 hours by eight hours/day, then I need a community educator for 30 days.

The above reasoning process is FAULTY for a number of reasons. What factors need to be considered when implementing a community education program for Geta Clinic? The following discussion will provide an example of the kind of "thinking-through" process needed to develop a more realistic estimate of the time it will take.

Access to the Community

Has the clinic ever provided educational programs in the schools? How much time will it take to develop the necessary relationships with the schools to gain access? How much time will be spent scheduling programs? How much time in community relations to develop the network? Will the sensitive nature of the topic impact on this development time by making it even more difficult to gain access to the classroom?

Service Preparation, Evaluation, and Documentation

How much preparation will be required to provide the educational program in addition to the direct teaching time? Will the educator need to write the curriculum? Will he/she also need to evaluate the program's effectiveness? Grade the evaluation exams? Maintain other program records? Develop handouts for classroom use?

Geographic Location

How many sites can be reached in a day? Consider the traffic patterns, distance, climate.

Ethnic, Cultural, Linguistic Considerations

Will the clinic need educators from different ethnic backgrounds? What languages will need to be spoken? Written? Is a special knowledge required to work with this specific population(s), and, if so, how much time will it take for the educator to acquire that?

Human Capability

Finally, consider what is humanly possible to require of a community educator in terms of actual teaching within a given day or week. The energy required in the classroom when the speaker is an "outsider" is considerably greater than when the audience is familiar with the person. Once the program has gained access to the schools, perhaps one 2-hour presentation per day is all you can reasonably expect someone to do and maintain enthusiasm in the process.

Putting It All Together

Now it is time to recalculate the amount of time required from the educational staff. A full-time employee works 2,080 hours per year. You have determined that the educator will need to spend time developing relationships with the schools. You might estimate that it will take approximately eight hours of contact time on the phone and in person per school that you want to reach. There are 50 high schools, and therefore, to contact each high school, it would entail about *400 hours*.

Then you calculate that it will take the educator approximately two to three weeks full time to review the materials that are available and to plan the curriculum. If portions of the curriculum need to be written or evaluation tools developed, it would take, you estimate, about one month, or *174 hours*.

We already know that the teacher will spend 240 hours in the classroom. He/she will go to 120 different classes, and let's say you estimate that it will take 30 minutes travel time each way, so that is another 120 hours in traveling time. So the time spent in classroom presentations and travel time totals *360 hours*.

You have also calculated that it will take the educator approximately one hour per class to handle the evaluation component, which equates to another **120 hours**. You want the educator to have a minimum of 10 hours per month to improve his/her skills and knowledge, to update records, attend an in-service, and respond to correspondence—which adds up to another *120 hours* for a total of *240 hours* for the evaluation.

Finally, let's add the fact that due to the sensitive nature of the materials to be addressed in the classroom, the community educator will also need to be involved in making a presentation at "Parent's Night," so that they may review materials and ask questions. This will require two hours at 50 schools for another *100 hours*, plus the one-hour travel time, for *50 hours*. There will be networking with other community groups, involvement on task forces or committees, which take another five hours per month or *60 hours* per year. That's a total of *210 hours*.

The total number of hours involved in the community educator's work comes to *1,384 hours for the project year*. There are 2,080 hours in a work year. Some planners will tell you that once you have made your best time estimate, it is wise to take an **additional 25%** or in this case an additional *520 hours*. The reasoning behind this is that things will always take more time than you think and there will inevitably be delays. In the case of the Geta Clinic, it appears that it would be wise to hire a full-time educator (100%) to reach 3,000 teens with an AIDS prevention program.

In the way that we have conceptualized the job now, the educator will spend the first four to five months preparing to teach and making contacts with the schools, and the remaining seven months of the project year providing the actual service. The factors we have included in calculating the amount of time an educator would spend to reach 3,000 teens should follow the implementation activities fairly closely. These calculations will also be needed as you determine the cost of the project. Often, as the true extent of time and effort needed are revealed, the implementation activities or the objectives may be modified to conform to budget restrictions.

Appendix B

Funding Resource Information

L isted below are common sources of information on funding resources that you might find helpful. This is a selective listing; for a more complete picture of funding opportunities, you can consult your local library or contact one of the following organizations/websites.

The University of Michigan

The University of Michigan's website offers access to funding sources, in-kind resources, electronic journals, how-to-guides, and other valuable resources.

Web address: www.ssw.umich.edu/resources/index2.html?collection=grants

The Grantsmanship Center

An organization that has an extensive inventory of funding information, publishes a newspaper for grant-seeking organizations, conducts national training on proposal writing and other areas of human service administration, conducts workshops on grant writing, offers consulting services, and offers a grant database.

Mailing Address: P.O. Box 17220; Los Angeles, CA 90017

Physical Address: 350 South Bixel St., Suite 110; Los Angeles, CA 90017

Web Address: www.tgci.com

The Foundation Center

An independent, national service organization established by foundations to provide an authoritative source of information on private philanthropic giving; publishes various directories and guides on foundations; and has established a national network of reference collections through local and university libraries, community foundations, and non-profit organizations.

Mailing Address: 79 Fifth Avenue/ 16th Street; New York, NY 10003

Web Address: www.foundationcenter.org

Internet Addresses of Selected Federal and State Funders

Catalog of Federal Domestic Assistance: www.cfda.gov

Grants.Gov: www.grants.gov

Housing and Urban Development Grants: www.hud.gov/grants

National Institutes for Health (NIH): www.nih.gov

Substance Abuse and Mental Health Services Administration: www.samhsa.gov

United States Department of Health and Human Services: www.dhhs.gov

United States Department of Education: www.ed.gov

Major Publications

Annual Register of Grant Support. Information Today, Inc., 143 Old Marlton Pike, Medford, NJ 08055.

Catalog of Federal Domestic Assistance. Superintendent of Documents, U.S. Government Printing Office, 732 North Capitol Street, NW, Washington, DC 20402.

Federal Grants and Contracts Weekly. John Wiley and Sons, Inc., 111 River Street, Hoboken, NJ 07030

Federal Register. Superintendent of Documents, U.S. Government Printing Office, 732 North Capitol Street, NW, Washington, DC 20402.

Publications of the Foundation Center, 79 Fifth Avenue/16th Street, New York, NY 10003

Foundation Directory

Foundation Directory Supplements

Foundation Grants to Individuals

National Directory of Corporate Giving

The Foundation Center's Guide to Proposal Writing

The Grantseeker's Guide to Winning Proposals

Foundation Fundamentals

Computerized Searches and Databases

There are a number of computerized search services available that provide funding resource information. The advantage of such databases is that they can subdivide and index the funding information into a range of subjects and categories (e.g., by subject, by geographic area). The costs can vary, and some of the information overlaps in the different databases. Check your local university library for more information about services. (Library tip: If you are no longer a student and want to use a university library, check to see if they have a "Friends of the Library" program. You may be able to join for a reasonable amount per year through this fundraising arm of the library.)

Dialog's *Information Retrieval Service* is among the largest databases covering a broad range of topics. Among the funding-related databases in the service are the following:

- Federal Register Abstracts
- Federal Research in Progress
- Foundation Directory
- Foundation Grants Index

Computerized searches are also useful for readily identifying literature and data for the need/problem statement section of the proposal. One might find journal articles or other educational resources at such sites as

- PsycINFO database
- ERIC
- EbscoHOST database: Social Science Abstracts
- Medline/PubMed
- Nexis Lexis

Online Journals and Newsletters

- Chronicle of Philanthropy: www.philanthropy.com
- Foundation News and Commentary: www.foundationnews.org/
- Grantsmanship Center Magazine: www.tgci.com/magazine.shtml

References and Suggested Readings

Bandura, A. (1986). *Social foundations of thought and action: A social cognitive theory*. Englewood Cliffs, NJ: Prentice Hall.

Brewer, E., Achilles, C., Fuhriman, J., & Hollingsworth, C. (2001). *Finding funding: Grantwriting from start to finish, including project management and internet use* (4th ed.). Thousand Oaks, CA: Corwin Press.

Burke, M. A. (2002). *Simplified grantwriting*. Thousand Oaks, CA: Corwin Press.

Diamond, H. (1998, July–August). A perfect union: Public–private partnerships can provide valuable services. *National Parks Forum, 72*(7–8), 41–42.

Dluhy, M., & Kravitz, S. (1990). *Building coalitions in the human services*. Newbury Park, CA: Sage.

Gardner, S. (1999). *Beyond collaboration to results: Hard choices in the future of services to children and families*. Arizona Prevention Resource Center: The Center for Collaboration for Children.

Kettner, P. M., & Martin, L. L. (1987). *Purchase of service contracting*. Newbury Park, CA: Sage.

Kettner, P. M., & Martin, L. L. (1996). *Measuring the performance of human service programs*. Newbury Park, CA: Sage.

Kettner, P. M., Moroney, R., & Martin, L. (2008). *Designing and managing programs: An effectiveness-based approach*. Thousand Oaks, CA: Sage.

Kiritz, N. J. (1980). *Program planning and proposal writing*. Los Angeles: The Grantsmanship Center.

Kniffel, A. (1995, November). Corporate sponsorship: The new direction in fundraising. *American Libraries, 26*(10), 1023–1026.

Knowlton, L., & Phillips, C. (2009). *The logic model guidebook: Better strategies for great results*. Thousand Oaks, CA: Sage.

Lauffer, A. (1997). *Grants, etc.: Grant getting, contracting and fund-raising for non-profits*. Thousand Oaks, CA: Sage.

Melaville, A. (1997). *A guide to selecting results and indicators: Implementing results-based budgeting*. Washington, DC: The Finance Project.

Netting, F. E., & Williams, F. G. (1997). Is there an afterlife? How to move towards self sufficiency when foundation dollars end. *Nonprofit management & leadership, 7*(3), 291–304.

127

Peterson, S. (2001). *The grantwriter's Internet companion*. Thousand Oaks, CA: Corwin Press.

Philanthropy. (n.d.). In *Online Etymology Dictionary*. Retrieved from Dictionary .com website: http://dictionary.reference.com/browse/philanthropy

Poor Law. (2012). In *Encyclopedia Britannica*. Retrieved from www.britanica .com/EBchecked/topic/469923/Poor-Law

Roth, J., Brooks-Gunn, J., Murray, L., & Foster, W. (1998). Promoting healthy adolescents: Synthesis of youth development program evaluations. *Journal of Research on Adolescents, 8*(4), 423–459.

Ruskin, K., & Achilles, C. (1995). *Grantwriting, fundraising, and partnerships: Strategies that work!* Newbury Park, CA: Corwin Press.

Schaefer, M. (1985). *Designing and implementing procedures for health and human services*. Beverly Hills, CA: Sage.

Schaefer, M. (1987). *Implementing change in service programs*. Newbury Park, CA: Sage.

Schorr, L. (1995). *The case for shifting to results-based accountability*. Washington, DC: Center for the Study of Social Policy.

Schram, B. (1997). *Creating small scale social programs*. Newbury Park, CA: Sage.

Soriano, F. I. (1995). *Conducting needs assessments: A multidisciplinary approach*. Newbury Park, CA: Sage.

Thayer, Kate. (2012, January 25). Hull house closing Friday. *Chicago Tribune*. Retrieved from http://articles.chicagotribune.com/2012-01-25/news/ct-met-hull-house-20120126_1_child-care-union-contract-employees

United Way of America. (1996). *Measuring program outcomes: A practical approach*. (4th ed.). Alexandria, VA: Author.

Vinter, R. D., & Kish, R. K. (1984). *Budgeting for not-for-profit organizations*. New York: Free Press.

Young, N., Gardner, S., & Coley, S. (1994). Getting to outcomes in integrated service delivery models. In *Making a difference: Moving to outcome-based accountability for comprehensive service reforms* (Resource Brief No. 7). Falls Church, VA: National Center for Service Integration.

Performance Indicators

Accreditation Council on Services for People with Disabilities. (1993). *Outcome based performance measures: A procedures manual*. Towson, MD: Author.

Annie E. Casey Foundation. (2011). *America's children, America's challenge: Promoting opportunity for the next generation*. (KIDS COUNT Data Book 2011). Baltimore, MD: Author.

Conoly, J., & Impara, J. *Mental measurements yearbook*. Lincoln, NE: Buros Institute of Mental Measurements.

Kumfer, K., Shur, G., Ross, J., Bunnell, K., Librett, J., & Millward, A. (1993). *Measurement in prevention: A manual on selecting and using instruments to evaluate prevention programs*. Washington, DC: Center for Substance Abuse Prevention, U.S. Department of Health and Human Services.

Touliatos, J., Perlmutter, B., & Straus, M. (1990). *Handbook of family measurement techniques*. Thousand Oaks, CA: Sage.

U.S. Department of Health and Human Services. (1994). *Assessing drug abuse among adolescents and adults: Standardized instruments* (Clinical Report Series). Rockville, MD: National Institute on Drug Abuse, Public Health Service.

Weiss, H., & Jacobs, F. (1988). *Evaluating family programs*. New York: Aldine de Gruyter.

Index

About the Authors

Soraya M. Coley is the provost and vice president for academic affairs at California State University, Bakersfield. She has over 25 years of academic and administrative experience, as well as extensive community service. She served as provost and vice president for academic affairs at Alliant International University, and as dean of the College of Human Development and Community Service at California State University, Fullerton.

Cynthia A. Scheinberg is a licensed clinical psychologist with over 23 years of administrative management in non-profit agencies. She has served as the executive director of the Coalition for Children, Adolescents and Parents (CCAP) in Orange, California; as senior vice president of clinical services for Anka Behavioral Health, Inc.; and as executive director of New Connections in Concord, California. She has a doctorate in clinical psychology from Pacifica Graduate Institute in Santa Barbara, California, and a master's degree in cultural anthropology from California State University, Fullerton. Dr. Scheinberg is now in private practice and consulting in Concord, California.

SAGE researchmethods

The essential online tool for researchers from the world's leading methods publisher

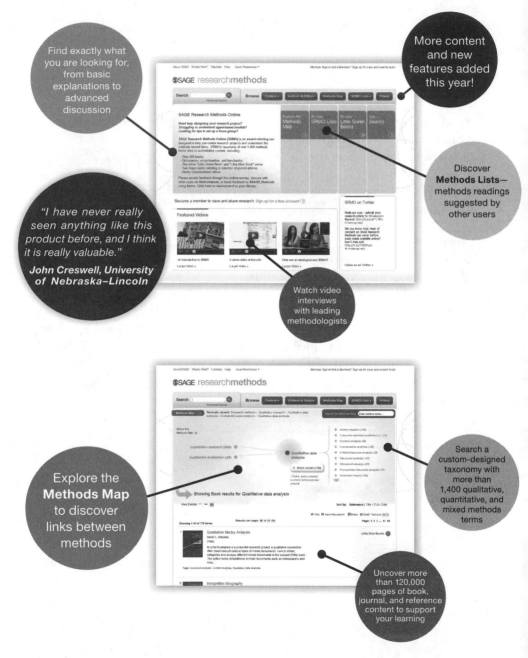

Find exactly what you are looking for, from basic explanations to advanced discussion

More content and new features added this year!

"I have never really seen anything like this product before, and I think it is really valuable."

John Creswell, University of Nebraska–Lincoln

Discover **Methods Lists**— methods readings suggested by other users

Watch video interviews with leading methodologists

Explore the **Methods Map** to discover links between methods

Search a custom-designed taxonomy with more than 1,400 qualitative, quantitative, and mixed methods terms

Uncover more than 120,000 pages of book, journal, and reference content to support your learning

Find out more at
www.sageresearchmethods.com